REALIZING MENTAL RESILIENCE

Tunde Ekpekurede

Unless otherwise indicated, all scripture quotations are taken from The Holy Bible, New International Version®, NIV® Copyright © 1973, 1978, 1984, 2011 by Biblica, Inc. ® Used by permission.
All rights reserved worldwide.

ISBN: 978-978-985-324-3

Edited by:
Miss Amai
Missamai.esq@gmail.com

Cover Design & Layout by:
Jerry Kanyinebi
Jerrykanyinebi01@gmail.com

Printed by:
Petbolgraphics
petbolgraphics@gmail.com

This book is Published by:

HRPS Limited
Consulting, Project Managers & Engineers
Tel: +447999 264036
E-mail: support@hrps.uk
URL: www.hrps.uk

To purchase bulk copies in paperback, please contact **support@learning4living.biz**

DEDICATION:

This book is dedicated to
Almighty God

Acknowledgement

I wish to acknowledge all those who have contributed in one way or the other towards the realization of this book in one form or the other. To my lovely wife, Faith for all the sacrifice and understanding in over 25 years of our marriage and my sounding board for most of what I have learnt on Realizing Mental Resilience. To all my children, Havilah, Rehoboth, Peniel & Samuel who have been one of my greatest teachers on Mental Resilience.

To all the Three Principles Practitioners who have helped my journey in this understanding - Tzvi Werther of the Twerski Wellness Institute, New Jersey who supported me in no small measure at the New Jersey immersion retreat of 2015. To all the "Three Principles Practitioners" whose writings and interactions have helped me in my journey to this understanding – Dr Amy Johnson, Dr Jack Pransky, Dr George Pransky, Dr Dicken Bettinger, Dr Bill Pettit, Micheal Neil, Damian Mark Smyth, Dr Keith Blevens, Steve Chandler, Laurie Holmes, Vicky Kelly, Pastor Abraham Ojeme, Belief Emadamerho and Garret Kramer amongst several others.

Special thanks to Kresta Laurel Limited for giving me two opportunities to demonstrate how the principles of resilience can be applied in driving organizational development, and to Lily Hospital for giving me the opportunity to use the resilience principles in this book to undertake executive coaching to some members of their management. Last but not the least, my special friend, Sam Egube who is always there, cheering me to victory.

Above all else, I give God all the glory for the inspiration to write this book

CONTENT

FOREWORD BY DAMIAN MARK SMYTH

Don't shoot the Messenger

What is the meaning of life? I can't tell you that, but I can tell you how you will find out if you get to be that fortunate... but you must promise not to shoot the Messenger, as the messenger will be you, and more specifically, your own thinking.

How can I say that 'You' will be the deliverer of such incredible insight, if and when it happens? 'We' give life meaning. And when I say we, I am using the collective term for the body of cells that make up the human form.

What unknown life force of nature gives power to this incredible array of orbiting electrons is way above my pay grade, but there can be no doubt that we're here, we're alive and we're experiencing something. Or you would not be reading this, and I could not have written it.

Thanks to the power of words, scribbled pictures that convey messages beyond the ink, we've been able to pass this down to others across generations of questioning and subsequently learning, how this 'stuff' actually works.

This is precisely what Tunde has done so beautifully in this latest documentation of a simple description which opens the doorway to more freedom than one could possibly imagine. As he so politely describes in his own view of my first written attempt in DO NOTHING! that has served him and his clients in a simple summation about how they were/are experiencing the world, via the power of thought.

This extra step is a subtle addition to the process but a crucial one, since there can be no experience of life without it, at least in human form, and to the best of our knowledge.

We (in this instance both Tunde and I) are putting what we know so far, into words, and pointing to something which is already there and has been there before language appeared in our armoury to share knowledge with others.

Life is energy. Energy has intelligence. Unless you stroll down to most middle town high streets at midnight on a Friday.

Perhaps best to stick with the intelligence of a system of, let's say, oaks in a forest forming a supportive ecosystem or the perpetual ability for 4800 new stars being created in the Universe every second to inflate themselves into planets and moons with orbits, from mere space dust.

Or my own attempt at creation, by forming obsessive-compulsive thoughts, as a protection system and strategy to keep me safe when I witnessed a traumatic event as a toddler. Thinking I could at first control, which later lost discipline like an unloved puppy.

Only later in life, seeing the system that we (humans) all use to create meaning out of anything, and spotting the innocence of my own strategy 'gone awry', and then being pointed back to the simplicity of the process and subsequently forgiving myself completely, allowed freedom from thought to emerge.

Tunde is allowing you to take a journey with him into how this thinking actually works. From self-awareness to listening to the deeper soul, better parenting to dealing with seductive thoughts, mental resilience, and dealing with adversity, to teenagers, marriage, relationships, and ordinary miracles…

I hope you, dear reader, whether you are new to this understanding of how you too (we all) create your/our experience from the inside out, via thought, brought to life via consciousness, or are a seasoned professional at picking out your own charlatan thoughts as the representation of your experience rather than the total true reality… I wish you a pleasant journey through this latest addition and hope it inspires you to take pen to paper to share your own stories, wisdom, and knowledge with others to make this best-kept secret, the norm in years to come.

ENDORSEMENTS

SAM EGUBE, Lagos State Commissioner for Budget & Economic Planning

Mental Resilience is the character of a person's mind in the face of living. It includes how the mind interprets life and is significantly influential in shaping the actual outcomes of our individual lives. Herein lies the difference between the life of one person and another.

Like a sparring partner, Tunde Ekpekurede stimulates our thinking and demonstrates that our reality is the craft of our mental creation. This book is a must read for resetting the way we engage life for victory.

MENA AJAKPOVI LLM (Bos) FCIArb (Lon), Partner, Udo Udoma & Bello Osagie

For anyone interested in finding a meaning to the varied circumstances of life, this book is a 'must read'. It is essentially a study guide in personal development and self-transformation, a riveting compendium of the experiences, analogies and horizons of eminent teachers and masters in this field. This book takes the subject from the realm of hypothesis, theories, and impracticable conjectures to the relatable day-to-day experiences and perceptions. You would not stop 'reading it till you finish reading it'. I attest to this, and I applaud Tunde for this very great work.

WOLE ABU, CEO Pan African Telecoms

The book is packed with practical wisdom from personal experience, contemporary research and some age-old wisdom. We are challenged to build an interior castle before doing it outside as the origin of all things is in the mind.

This is a great and timely work coming upon the stage at this time, when uncertainty and fear seem to rule the world and bad news is the mainstream media's portrait of the world.

This is a book about hope, resilience and succeeding with the tools that are already within us. An excellent read, written in simple direct language and manageable chapters, you can start from anywhere and get a nugget of wisdom. This should be in everyone's glove box. Take it around with you and don't leave it on the bookshelf because it's a manual for living in today's world.

ENGR. DIDEOLU FALOBI, FNSE, FIoD, CEO, Kresta Laurel Limited

Realising Mental Resilience is an eye-opening guide into the depth of our mental capabilities and how we can maximize its potentials. Through Tunde's personal yet enlightening stories, you will begin to embrace better thinking. Each chapter, a breath of fresh air, a wave of new knowledge, a change in our perception/thinking, bringing you to a general Eureka Moment!

DR AUSTIN OKOGUN, CEO Lily Hospitals Group

This book vividly captures the inherent and potent power that is available to everyone for dealing with all of life's challenges.
Drawing from practical life experiences and inspiring stories, the author lays out a strong argument for achieving the best out of life through self-realization and awareness.

A must read for everyone who desires success in all endeavours through understanding the wonders of the most powerful 'AI' ever made- the human mind. I strongly recommend it for leaders and all aspiring leaders to be.

INTRODUCTION

MY JOURNEY TO THIS BOOK

I finished my MBA studies from the University College, Dublin, and Republic of Ireland in August 2004. From August 2004 till June 2010, I worked in eight different organizations, changing jobs seven times. This simply means that I was holding one job every 10 months on the average. Looking back, I was fortunate to have changed jobs with such amazing ease, but this also meant severe stress for my family and me.

Children attended more schools than they could count. In some cases, attending a school for less than a term before moving to a new city. To help you understand the changes in my life from this experience, all job switches except one involved moving from one city to another and in three cases moving from one country to another. In two of these job changes, I had just taken out mortgages and bought beautiful family homes with a promise to my family that "this is going to be the final bus stop". As it turned out, both bus stops lasted six months each.

In the Republic of Ireland, I abandoned a pricey 4 bed duplex and jumped ship after just six months of living in this palatial home - I moved to England. Fascinated by the beauty and warmth of East Sussex, I took out another mortgage and bought a 5-bed home in Eastbourne and declared it my very final bus stop. Six months after moving into this beautiful home, I resigned my job as General Manager of Stonerbenton Precast Limited and took up another job as General Manager, Titan Precast Limited in Northern Ireland. Just when my children were settling into new friendships, we were gone. I remember all the efforts my daughter, Havilah, expended to gain admission into

East Sussex College, Eastbourne in 2007, two months after celebrating, we were on a one-way ticket to Belfast, Northern Ireland.

I managed to always see the ease with which I moved from one executive job to another as a show of strength and testament to my managerial prowess – Truth is that some work pressure was becoming unbearable and I was justified to move. Even when my family suffered financially after the 8th job change, I still did not see what I could improve at.

I urged my wife to move back to the UK where she could work as a medical doctor and earn better wages to sustain the school fees of the kids. I turned my energies to teaching unemployed graduates employability skills - a hunger I have felt for a while during these years. This passion soon affected several hundred graduates who were attending my employability classes and getting gainful employment. I created modules for companies and several companies signed up.

As I hungered and laboured passionately to teach everything I knew about management, (I was going through a lot of emergency trainings to be able to teach some of the courses) I began to see myself in some of the participants. As I facilitated each class, sometimes facilitating six hours of management training in one day, I began to learn just as much or perhaps more than the managers that came to my classes.

One of my mentors, the late Jim Rohn, says that one advantage of speaking and lecturing is that when you speak in ten different classes, you get to hear the same message preached, ten different times. I grew faster in these classes than all the lectures I received in my MBA program.

I remember in one personal development class for managers, as we discussed the good and the bad reasons for resignations, I was frozen in my tracks when I realized that I should not have jumped ship in my last resignation and that the pressures for which I blamed my last boss was more of a weakness on my part and not my boss.

This realization increased my hunger to help participants of the program avoid the errors I made even though I still did not have a concise way of helping them know what to do if they found themselves in my position.

I bought several management cases studies from the Harvard Business Review. The good thing I enjoyed in facilitating a class is that you did not need to always come out as a subject expert to facilitate. As I facilitated class after class, I improved professionally and in my ability to facilitate classes. The participants gained tremendously. I like participatory classes a lot as it affords participants the opportunity to hear much more varied views of the same subject. I immersed myself in a great deal of studies spending substantial amounts on the acquisition of knowledge during this period.

In 2014, during one of those hungry searches on how I might better the experience of participants who attended my classes, I hopped from one reference material to another, I stumbled onto a book, "THE MIND MADE PRISON" by Mateo Tabatabai. This book showed me the role of our thinking in our experience of life in a way I never knew before. After reading this book, I researched references and persons mentioned in it, including related subject searches and in the course of my search I came across a body of knowledge called "The Three Principles", www.3pgc.org and one of its notable authors, Damian Mark Smyth, author of the book "DO NOTHING".

I immediately bought a Kindle copy of "DO NOTHING". As I read the book, I experienced a level of understanding of how we use our thinking to inflict stress on ourselves beyond what words could describe. I would later buy over 10 copies of the book "DO NOTHING" and distribute to friends and relatives. Also, I bought extra copies of the book, kept some at home and gave them out to persons who came to me for counselling.

By January 2015, providing training to individuals and organizations had taken a greater portion of my time. In late January, I decided to invest in myself by attending one of largest gathering of trainers and facilitators in Atlanta, USA. Aside the conferences, I paid for a weeklong "TRAIN THE TRAINER" certification course. On my last day of my stay in Atlanta, I received an email from a THREE PRINCIPLES ORGANIZATION I had subscribed to that there was a conference coming up in New Jersey just a week after my departure from Atlanta.

I certainly could not miss this opportunity, so I changed my travel plans back to Nigeria, rescheduled prior engagement and made reservations at the Sheraton Four Point Hotel in New Jersey, venue of the conference. The three-day conference was quite refreshing. Aside the understanding I gained at the conference, I acquired a box load of books and audio materials and returned to Nigeria.

Since 2015, I have had numerous opportunities to share my knowledge of this understanding of how our life experiences are created with individuals and organizations. I have attended numerous trainings and conferences including one with Butterfly Effect Coaching, "State of

Mind & Performance" facilitated by Garret Kramer and Vicky Kelly in April 2018 and LIFE 2.0 conference in North London, July 2018, which I attended with my lovely wife. In 2019, I attended Michael Neill's "The Advanced Courses 4.0" I have also invested a great deal of time watching several YouTube sessions to deepen my understanding of how our life experience is formed.

This book is my attempt to put to paper, much of what I have learned during these years in the field of peak performance, mental resilience, staying power and relationships. The understanding espoused in this book will bring the most disillusioned at work, in life, in marriage, in school, in any walk of life to a peace previously unknown. The book is meant for persons of all ages, for primary school kids as well corporate CEOs and presidents. Application of this understanding has been employed in business, groups, entrepreneurs, and families to unleash the highest potentials of individuals and teams in every kind of context.

I was with an executive director of a quoted company shortly after my return to Nigeria in 2015, his sleeping pattern was severely impacted by the operating results of his company that year. I spent 3 hours with this executive and gave him a copy of Damian Mark Smyth's book, "DO NOTHING". By the 3rd day, this executive had regained his strength and was back to work, fully engaged and motivated, despite no change in the company performance. He was also back sleeping as normal just after 3 days and cancelling all prior appointments to see a counsellor.

In several conferences and seminars, I have witnessed the awesome potential that this understanding holds for humanity and I hope with this publication, I have made a little contribution to this understanding and the many lives that shall come in contact with this book.

Chapter One

Creating Meanings That Empower You: Realizing Mental Resilience

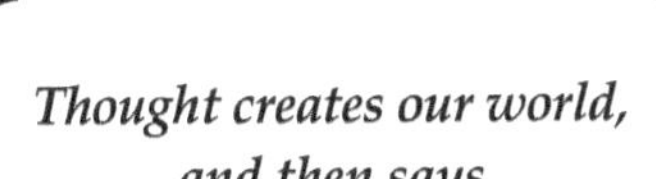

*Thought creates our world,
and then says
'I didn't do it" – David Bohn*

There are no identical twins anywhere in the world with the same experience of their mother/father/sibling or life in general. We can build a hypothetical case and assume that these twins, now 20 years of age ate the same food, received the same treatment in school, at home and everywhere we might imagine. The question is: why is it so? The answer is simply because we do not experience life from the external environment, we experience life from the INSIDE OUT. Two people can look at the same thing and make different meanings out of it.

The real work that humans are engaged with every day is MEANING MAKING. We are expert Meaning Makers, but the greatest tragedy of life is that we are not aware that we are the ones making the meaning. We look at the same thing and we make different meanings out of it. I wish to show you in this short write up that whether you are sad or happy, it is the result of the meaning you are making in the current moment about life. Your perception of your office boss right now, is a meaning you created.

Last year in a WhatsApp group that I belong to, a fellow made a video posting which left me terrified after watching it and thoughts about the video kept me awake nearly all night. However, there were people making comments about the video and were having fun. So, what was happening there? We were all making different meanings from the same video. I might say that the video kept me awake all night, but if the video had the power to keep anyone awake all night, it certainly would have kept everyone awake all night. The reality is that I was making meaning from the video that terrified me.

Two people are working in the same company and for one person the company is a terrible place to work, for another person, there can be no better place to work. Two persons are having identical challenges in marriage, while one is having his/her best time in life, the other is considering committing suicide. A surprising thing is that if you interview both persons, you will find out that both are tracing their experience to the same issue and yet they are having different experiences in life. The problem is that both are ignorant of the greatest and most subtle deceit of life. We are the ones making meaning of the event.

We make meaning and **THINK** about the meaning we are making; and once we **THINK** about the meaning we **EXPERIENCE** the thoughts we have in the moment. If the thought is one that is good, we experience good feelings and if the thought is bad, we experience bad feelings. As an engineer, I remember standing on top of the roof of a tall building; when I moved close to the edge of the building my heart began racing at the speed of light. On that roof, there was a carpenter with me who was standing at the edge of the parapet wall and smoking. I never dared near the parapet wall. I was **THINKING** of how my life will come to an end once I fall off the tip of the building. The carpenter wasn't **THINKING** what I was thinking, so he was having a different experience. I might conclude that the height of the roof was what was terrifying me, but the reality was that I was making meanings from the height, which in turn terrified me.

In 2016, I was reading the newspaper and I read of young girls who were raped in the Syrian war, they could not stand the trauma of being raped and committed suicide. The next day, I was watching another documentary of the Syrian civil war on television where some young Syrian girls who were violently raped by Syrian soldiers were helping others escape from the city of Aleppo, Syria. From both stories, the survivors were given a far worse treatment than those that committed suicide. What was the difference? The difference was that both sets of girls made different meanings from the incident.

The point here isn't the morality of being raped, it is the meaning that we make out of every day events that happen to us. Once we **WAKE UP** to the reality that we are the ones making the meaning of everyday events, we will be **FREE**. We will find out that we are architects of our own lives and we will **INTENTIONALLY** change the meanings we make in life.

I recall a story told by Anthony Robbins in his book, **AWAKEN THE GIANT**, about two brothers born of the same parents. While one was a drunkard and depressed, the other was an executive in a company and happy with his life. When both were interviewed, the depressed one narrated how he grew up in a home where his father, who was a drunkard and who died depressed, physically abused his mum every day. He concluded his story by saying "what do you expect from me after growing up in that kind of environment?"

Anthony Robbins wondered what the other brother knew that gave him a different/happy outcome. When the brother was interviewed he told the very same story that his brother told, but his conclusion was different. In his conclusion, he said "every day I came home and witnessed my father physically abusing my mother, I said to myself, **MY LIFE WILL NEVER END LIKE THIS**".

Irrespective of any situation we find ourselves in life, the key to happiness is the realization that **I AM THE ONE MAKING THE MEANING**. What I am trying to say is that if you are having an unpleasant experience of life right now, you can change the experience by changing the meaning that you are making in the moment.

Chapter Two

Creating Meanings That Empower You: 2 Realizing Mental Resilience

> *Thought creates our world,*
> *and then says 'I didn't do it"*
> *– David Bohn*

The e-mail you got from your boss yesterday had no meaning, until you gave it your unique meaning. The text message you just read on your phone had no meaning until you assigned one to it. Your boss's refusal to return your call had no meaning until you gave it one. The news that your company will be laying off 20% of its staff had no meaning until you gave it one. The competitor moving in across the street meant nothing, until you give it meaning. The downturn in the market meant nothing, until you created a meaning for it, therefore, all these feelings that go against your success have been caused by your thoughts, not by any event or news. Your spouse not picking your call for the last three hours meant nothing, until you gave it your meaning. So, the other driver cut in on you in traffic in the wrong way and that has unsettled your emotions. Really? Events have no life in themselves. Even the "brutal murder" you just saw on television had no meaning until you gave it one.

"We, as a collective culture, have bought into the belief that events and people can make us feel and act a certain way. This belief is the biggest obstacle to having an **OK** business, an **OK** career, an **OK** marriage, a fantastic innovative business and a blissful life.

Events cannot cause feelings because they do not have that power. It's not really how the brain works. The biological computer processes thoughts. That's it. That's all. Thoughts. Nothing else.

*It is always and only processing your thoughts. It is not processing "situations". It only feels that way. But it also "feels like" the earth is flat and it "feels like" the sun goes away at night. We misinterpret a lot! Until we don't. And once we don't, the biocomputer can now be used for what it was intended to be used for: to get you what you really want. Question your thinking." - **Richard Habets***

Since learning this subtle trick of how life works, I have experienced greater resilience in my personal life. I have gone through some personal life situations that would have really caused my feet to slip if they happened before I practiced these principles.

Not long ago, I needed to be completely undressed for a medical examination. My wife, who is a doctor and worked in the same hospital, began working the politics of the hospital to ensure that a male doctor examined me. She told me stories of patients who chose to go home when a doctor of the same sex was not available to carry out a similar examination.

In one heart - rending story she narrated from working at a previous hospital, she told me of a woman who was supposed to be examined for cancer of the cervix but refused to be examined even by a female doctor, insisting that only her husband can get access to certain parts of her body. Despite pleas from other female medical officers, this woman would not yield; she finally died refusing treatment. Back to my appointment, my wife played the politics well and got me a male doctor to examine me. Owing to what I know about making meanings, I could not care less about who examined me. If there was no male doctor on duty, I would have insisted to be seen by any female doctor that was available. The issue isn't who examines me, the issue is the meaning I make from the event.

No two people work in the same company with the same experience of the company. As expert meaning makers, we are always trying to second guess people. I remember working in a company some years ago. I enjoyed a particularly good working relationship with my boss *(Now I can see that I was the one making the meaning and I am glad I made positive meanings)*. Then suddenly, my boss will not stop by my office as before. My mind started racing from one event to the other.

This situation went on for nearly two weeks. My blood pressure was rising. I tried to find out from a few colleagues if they were experiencing any sudden change of behaviour from the boss, but I was shocked that they had no clue what I was talking about. They could not see sense in what I was feeling. The more these negative thoughts wrapped me, the greater the seeming distance between me and the boss.

I got home and told my wife that I seem to have fallen out of favour with my boss. I rang a company that earlier offered me a job which I turned down and told them I was willing to take up the job. They immediately sent me a new offer, though with improved pay, but less than my current pay. Armed with an alternative offer, I privately went to see my boss in his office to be sure everything was OK.

He seemed baffled by some of the questions I asked him. During the conversation, I would come to find out that my boss was going through an exceedingly difficult domestic challenge and was in fact thinking of increasing my responsibilities temporarily. The meanings I created got me screwed.

The seeming silence and distance that you are perceiving from your buddies, means nothing until you give it your unique meaning. The omission of your name from the list of invited guests in that party, means nothing until you give it your unique meaning.

There is an interesting story in the Bible of how a king **CREATED NEGATIVE MEANING FROM A SUPPOSEDLY POSITIVE SITUATION USING THE MEANING MAKING POWER OF THINKING.** The Story is in 1Chronicles 19: 1-4. "In the course of time, Nahash king of the Ammonites died, and his son succeeded him as king. 2 David thought, "I will show kindness to Hanun son of Nahash, because his father showed kindness to me." So David sent a delegation to express his sympathy to Hanun concerning his father.

When David's envoys came to Hanun in the land of the Ammonites to express sympathy to him, 3 the Ammonite commanders said to Hanun, "Do you think David is honoring your father by sending envoys to you to express sympathy? Haven't his envoys come to you only to explore and spy out the country and overthrow it?" 4 So Hanun seized David's envoys, shaved them, cut off their garments at the buttocks, and sent them away.

David wanted to do the King good; but the King and his subjects **THOUGHT** otherwise. Read from verse 4 to see the destruction that a wrong thinking created.

What meanings are you making from your current situation?
What meanings are you making in your current relationships or workplace?

You can use your thinking to create **PAIN** or **HAPPINESS**. The decision is yours, **ALWAYS!**

Chapter Three

Happy Innocence Day

> *"We were once like children,*
> **UNAWARE** *before we became*
> *adults, before we became*
> **AWARE**." –
> *Tunde Ekpekurede*

May 27 is children's day. As usual you get to see lots of Happy Children's day greetings and posters. One greeting struck me among the many that I received this year; it was titled **HAPPY INNOCENCE DAY**. It got me thinking. If the celebration of children is the celebration of innocence, I imagined that the celebration of adults has to be the opposite. So, what is the opposite of innocence, I reasoned. I went to the online dictionary to find out the meaning of the word innocence and it says *"guiltless, freedom from moral wrong, freedom from moral or specific wrong. Webster says **the state of being unaware or uniformed**"*. I got it. Our lives were once like children's before we became adults, before we became **AWARE**.

When we were born, we were **UNAWARE** of anything in this physical world. We just emerged from another world. The survival strategies in this new world looked different from where we came from. We needed to quickly learn. So, we started learning. We began coding our brains as we were growing. When we mistakenly put our hands in the fire, it burnt us, so we decided we will never do it again. We wrote it in the cells of our brain. We were given this storage notebook called brain to write whatever we wanted to write. This way we do not have to wake up every morning to try and remember the name of our parents. Every person living in the world has a unique mental diary.

Today scientists say everyone has a unique **DNA**. When we made these mental notes called beliefs, it was intended to help us navigate life; to learn, to adapt and these beliefs or memories were there to protect us. Immediately we encounter any situation, our beliefs immediately tell us what to do. This is what artificial intelligence **(AI)** is trying to replicate right now. By loading billions and trillions of scenario-based events and responses, **AI** is trying to create a supercomputer that will beat man. Enough of AI today – maybe some other day.

Like **AI**, our beliefs have become a supercomputer that we built, both consciously and unconsciously. We wrote in it everything that we thought will give us a happy life and that is what we are using every day to run our lives. We learnt from various sources and made our individual conclusions from the inside of us. For example, when lady A sees lady B happy because lady B's husband or boyfriend celebrated her birthday, lady A may have unconsciously wrote in the slate of your mind that "I will be happy when my boyfriend celebrates my birthday".

You saw that a person looked happy when they had N1m in the bank and you wrote in your brain that "N1m bank balance makes me happy". You wrote in your brain that "a lady should be married by 25 otherwise her value as a lady begins to diminish". You wrote in your brain that life will be miserable if as a man you have not bought your first car at 30. You wrote in your brain that a man ought to have finished his first degree by 25. You were the one who wrote in your brain that "A man's income ought to be higher than that of his wife".

It was you and I that wrote in our brains how we will know if our bosses like us. We wrote in our brains what our parents needed to do for us to feel loved as children. On and on, there are probably thousands, if not millions of known and unknown beliefs in your brain, many of which you are not even aware of until you encounter the situation where your supercomputer needs to pull it out.

What is the implication of all these artificial intelligence that you have built up? They are **ONLY** true in your internal interpretation of life. **THEY ARE NOT REALITY**. No two persons have their brains configured the same way. So, when you get to the office and your boss has a "weird" look – (remember that a weird look is defined by your internal computer – there is no good or bad look in itself), your **AI** immediately begins to sound a warning alert- danger, danger, danger. You are terrified. You convince yourself that you are being terrified by your boss's looks when your **AI** is what is terrifying you. You learnt from other kids in school what it means for your father to be loving, and when you get home, your father displays a different algorithm. What happens next? Your **AI** begins to scream **"My father does not love me"**. You unconsciously begin to hate him; you resent him and openly speak evil of him. One child gets to school and tells other kids of how her father took her to the cinema on children's day and all the love she experienced. Another kid hears this and her computer processes all the flogging she got from her dad on children's day for not washing the dishes. She cannot believe that she will be treated this "bad" **"ON A SPECIAL DAY"** like this.

She writes in her computer, "**MY FATHER IS WICKED**". In today's modern world she goes to social media to see what other kids are doing who also think that their fathers do not love them, and they too begin to do it. I can go on and on and fill a book on different scenarios that we have created in our computer that defines who we are. I will rather stop here and allow you to do the introspection yourself and come up with all the coding inside you.

Is there anything wrong with any of these algorithms in our supercomputer? Absolutely **NOTHING**. Here is the challenge, **NOT ALL OF THESE CODES ARE SERVING YOU**. Some of these codes served your interest well at a specific time in your life but are no longer serving you. Think of a computer today running an operating system developed 40 years ago. It cannot communicate in today's operating system – it needs to be updated. Today, most devices and gadgets are automatically updating their software once they are connected to the internet. You too should be checking your software.

20 years ago, after a terrible relationship break up, you wrote in your **AI** that all men were devils. Is that belief still relevant today? The belief helped you overcome a difficult time in your life then, but is it still serving your needs for today? You lost your job in a power tussle with a person from a different ethnicity or race and wrote in your **AI** that all men from that ethnicity cannot be trusted. Does that belief still serve you today? When you lost your job that belief may have been temporarily necessary (wrong or right) to help you make meaning of the event and move on, but you did not delete it after you got your next job. Now, that belief is warning you of danger since a person from that ethnicity was appointed your new boss. Do

you still think the belief is necessary? I am not here to tell you which belief is good and which belief is bad. There isn't anything like that. The question is, **"Is this belief serving my happiness?"**.

You see, as we mature, we move from innocence to awareness. I am an amateur in reading the Bible, but I like this quote from Romans 5:13, "For sin was in the world before the Law was given; but sin is not taken into account when there is no law". Part B of that verse says sin is not **_considered_** when there is no law. Nothing can terrify you except it goes against an ingrained belief (coding) or **LAW.** If there is no belief on the subject, you will scarcely be aware if the event happened because your supercomputer will not even pick it.

All over the world, laws are being updated. The United State's Government has just rolled back the tough banking regulations that were imposed in the aftermath of the collapse of Lehmann Brothers. Why? Because it is no longer serving the country. You see, you are only terrified by what is contrary to your computer programming. Since no two people have the same computer programming, we are not all terrified by the same event. Even when we may both be terrified by the same event; the severity may be ranked differently in our **AI.** One person is only mildly stressed by an event, the second person is already heading to a psychiatric hospital as his **AI** programming has crashed. In security parlance one person classified the risk at level 5 security threat, while another merely placed it on level 1 and for another it has been delisted. Do an introspection and see which beliefs look like level 1. If they serve your interest then it is OK, but if they do not, you may want to downgrade the level of security threat, update it with a new belief or just delete it.

I have seen marriages where a husband forgetting the wife's birthday is classed as a level 5 threat and as soon as the husband forgets the birthday, the marriage is ripped apart by the response of the wife. If you interview the woman she will put a lot of sentiments into what happened on that day: that her husband forgot her birthday and she just could not comport herself, so she lost her cool, and on and on - the story will never end. I am sure there are marriages where the woman even forgets her own birthday let alone that of the spouse. So, what ripped the marriage apart was not that the husband forgot the birthday, but the ___*meanings*___ surrounding the birthday for the woman might just have been set at a level 5 threat.

If you are fine ripping apart the marriage for this reason, well and good, but if you are not fine and you think the possibility does exist for your spouse to forget your birthday, and you do not want to give a level 5 threat reaction, you may want to downgrade the threat level in your supercomputer. I was in church a while ago and the pastor said, "no man who loves his wife will forget the wife's birthday". I said to myself, that is just half-truth. Birthdays are not **REALITY**. Every day is the same and everyday can become what you want it to be. You can choose to celebrate your wife every day. In the real world, there is no time. Where you originated from has no time. Time is a concept but we will get to that later.

Have you considered that this might just be a good time to have a check on some of your **NO GO AREAS** in your belief system?

Chapter Four

Dealing with Guilt & Shame – Realizing Mental Resilience

> *The problem is not your thinking.*
> *The problem is believing that your feelings*
> *are coming from something other than*
> *your thinking in that moment. Feelings,*
> *experience, reality is being created always,*
> *only, this one way."* – **Valda Monroe**

In April 2017, a 100 level **UNILAG** (University of Lagos, Nigeria) student committed suicide. According to the story carried by the Punch Newspaper and several other dailies, "Aribiyi Ayomide has reportedly taken her own life after she was shamed publicly by her roommates". The 100 level Employee & Human Relations Management Student was accused by her roommates of stealing their "make ups" and clothing. When her mother came to rescue her, her roommates booed her, calling her all sorts of names to shame her. On getting home and thinking of all the shame of going back to school, Ayomide decided to take her own life.

When I read the story, I was really "sad". How can you take your life for something that does not exist? **SHAME ONLY EXISTS IN THE MIND OF THE PERSON EXPERIENCING IT.** Shame is self-created. 98% of people in psychiatric homes today are there because of a fundamental misunderstanding of how life works. There is nothing called shame. When we are caught up with this misunderstanding of how our moment-to-moment experience of life is formed, we erroneously fall for these deadly preys.

Last week an avid reader of my articles on this subject called to discuss a difficulty she was having at her place of work in one of these banks in Victoria Island, Lagos Nigeria. As it turned out, she narrated how her boss talks to her in the presence of other staff members and how she gets embarrassed. She went on to say that she was considering resigning her job. I told her in no emotional terms that the embarrassment she claimed was not reality. She argued that her colleagues looked at her a certain way after the so-called embarrassment. I said to her, you are the one that created the so-called embarrassment. There is no event in this world that has the capacity to make you ashamed or embarrassed unless you permit it.

Just last week, the gossip mills were awash with the rumour that a Nigerian lady had jumped into the lagoon and taken her life as her infidelity was to become a matter of public knowledge. Unable to stand the shame, she decided to end her life. I was "sad" reading this gossip. How and why should one end their life, leaving 3 kids behind for a self-created **THOUGHT** that **DOES NOT EXIST**. Let me expatiate here, these meditations are not about what is moral or what is immoral, rather, they are meant to explain **EXACTLY HOW LIFE WORKS**. The infidelity is a fact. The infidelity happened.
The SHAME IMAGINED DOES NOT EXIST.

Take the 100 level **UNILAG** student, if she understood life at the level of consciousness in which I am writing (you see, I wasn't always at this level of consciousness; I will say that I lost half of my life to this ignorance. If I knew what I am teaching today before I was 20, my life will be far richer and better than what it is today), she could consider the following options. My thievery has been brought to light. I am going to stop this thievery. I am going to meet my roommates and apologize that this **WILL NEVER** happen again. I am going to let them know that I need help with clothing and I will be very glad if there is any way that they can be of help. I am going to tell them that going forward they have my permission to search my belongings without my knowledge. I am going to tell them that I will work on this habit of thievery and that it is a habit that has been with me for a while and I really need their help to overcome it. What do you think will be the response of her roommates to a conversation like this? I leave the guess to you my readers. Personally, I will suspect that the roommates will show a lot of compassion towards her and decide to help her going forward. I will suspect that the roommates will fall in love with her and support her socially, academically and morally.

The next question is, can she have this conversation? For 999 out of 1000 teenagers living today, this conversation is **IMPOSSIBLE**. The reason is that "Ego", a self-destruct "outside -in" concept of who we think we are has created a barrier in our subconscious programming. There are millions, if not billions of people today who are in one difficulty or another because of **EGO**. There are people today who should still be employed if they were willing to say **SORRY** and despise their **INTERNAL THINKING**. Let's even assume that the roommates are so wicked that even after her apology, they continue to shame her. At my current level of consciousness, I will advise her to change rooms. If this is not possible, she should come to school from home. But you see, when **EGO** is mixed with a misunderstanding of how life works, she will think that this is something impossible to do.

SHAME tells you everyone is aware of your problem when you are the **ONLY** one aware of your problem. **SHAME** tells you people are talking about you when in reality people are so busy with their lives they hardly remember that you exist. For goodness sake, **UNILAG** has over 30,000 students, only 3 of your roommates know of your crime. Let's assume the 3 roommates do a good gossip work and take the news to 100 persons each, which works out to be 300 persons. For goodness sake 300 persons out of 30,000 students is less than 1% of the entire student population.

Even in this odd reasoning that I have done, let's even assume that all 30,000 **UNILAG** students knew of the crime. To tell you the truth, until you create an event in your mind, it doesn't exist, not even when 30,000 students know about what you did. When you are alone in your mother's house, you aren't sleeping with 30,000 people; you are sleeping with **ONLY ONE THING – YOUR THOUGHTS**. When everyone is long gone, when you have even succeeded in graduating from **UNILAG**, the incidence could still exist in your thinking. What do you do at this stage? The answer is **NOTHING**. You do not do anything about thoughts. Thoughts are just what they are. They are thoughts. Nothing more. At even a low level or reasoning, if you are not deluded by consciousness, you will change university; unless you are such a psychiatric wreck to think that 170million Nigerians are thinking of you.

The day you find out that you are not as important as your **EGO** tells you that you are, the quality of your life will improve by at least 50%. The man Kenneth Copeland is one of the greatest gospel preachers alive today. I was listening to him one day and he made this statement "If I find newspaper headlines in Texas tomorrow saying that I am the biggest fraud in Texas, it won't make a dent on who I am for one moment - I just go on to honour my next assignment". You see, a lot of people have an inflated view of themselves. So, knowledge of your infidelity is coming into public domain. Hey madam, we don't even know you. We are so busy with our lives we could not care less. If Donald Trump's alleged infidelity could not stop him from becoming the president of the United States, it will amount to delusion to end your life for infidelity or anything whatsoever.

As an **NYSC** corps member in Kano in 1990, I was a member of the "Christian Corpers Fellowship" and was privileged to preach on forgiveness one day. Soon after my message, news reached us that a fellow Christian corps member who was serving in another state had committed suicide because he committed fornication – the sin of sex before marriage. My friend and brother Charles Iwuagwu who listened to my message on God's forgiveness said, "Tunde will never commit suicide because he committed fornication". You see, I could not in my young age imagine that God will refuse to forgive me for a sin I committed because I was already a Christian, when I knew that He was forgiving murderers who were not even His children every day.

As a teenager, I bothered a lot about what people thought about me; in my late thirties I bothered less, in my forties, I never bothered about what anyone thought about me anymore. Guess what, in my fifties, I found out that nobody was thinking about me all along. Your experience of life exists only in your thoughts. Nothing else. Not knowing that this is the way life works has sent so many innocent people to their graves. Many have lost careers, relationships and families.

My experience of life exists **ONLY** in my thoughts. My thoughts can only harm me when I give them the power to do so. To give them the power, I must hold on to them and affirm them. Hey, stop that habit of worrying. I am not my thoughts and I am just going to party all night. Will you join me?

Chapter Five

The Principle of Separate Realities

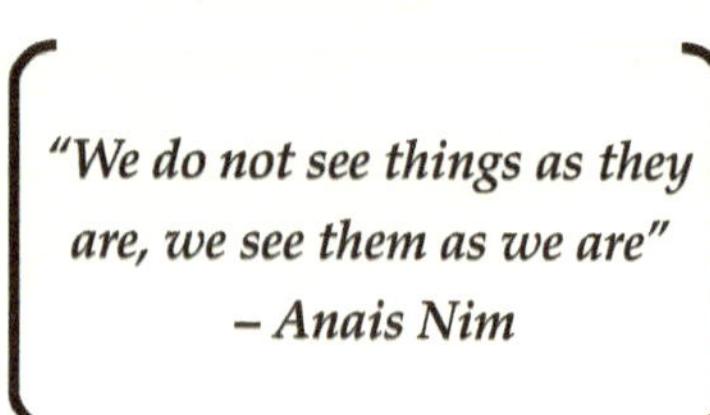

The greatest error in our understanding of life is that there is only one reality at any given time in a given situation. Even in politics, there isn't any single interpretation of reality. If you want to be successful in relationships of any kind, you have to go beyond tolerating people; you have to understand that in any given situation and event there are millions of realities being created by the millions of persons observing the event.

The Principle of Separate Realities simply says that no two individuals have the same reality of any given event. Amateur counsellors are amazed when they listen to people in dispute and hear different narrations on the same issue in dispute. We live in separate silos of thoughts that we have created that we call reality. Our default thinking should be to expect that people will see things different from the way we do. I can see that if we can rewire our brain to this position we would have eliminated over 50% of the difficulties experienced in relationships. This simple mental reset will bring a lot of love and understanding into our day to day conversations. It will remove a lot of the ego we bring into conversations and help us forge better and lasting relationships. When people travel to foreign countries, they immense themselves in experiencing the new culture and seeing the amazing differences in the people, places and food. We ought to likewise watch people who are close to us or colleagues at work or spouses with that same awe and fun when they express their reality in any given situation. Our ability to do this will significantly transform any relationship.

"There is nothing either good or bad in itself but thinking makes it so."
William Shakespeare, Hamlet

Romans 14:14 "I am convinced and fully persuaded in the Lord Jesus that nothing is unclean in itself. But if anyone regards something as unclean, then for him it is unclean."

In Shakespeare's Hamlet, when Hamlet calls Denmark a prison, he is mentally and physically confined by the gaze of the king and his agents, and he feels trapped in the court's general degradation—"Something is rotten in the state of Denmark," he moans; but he is just a prisoner of his own thinking. How many people have pronounced their jobs, situations or life in general a prison, when all they are seeing is their thinking?

The greatest pain we can experience in life isn't the lack of money, it is the painful meanings we give to the events of our lives.

We experience pain because our meanings of every day event do not line up with our expectations of life or beliefs. When we expect that there will be no traffic and we come across traffic on our way to work, we begin to cuss and get stressed out. The reality is that the traffic is just made of some inanimate objects called cars, with no power to make any meaning or get anyone stressed. Some other person in the same traffic is rejoicing because he needed the traffic to slow him down as he was arriving for a scheduled place of meeting too early. The traffic has nothing to do with the experience of life of any of these persons. They gave it whatever meaning depending on their internal beliefs or expectations.

"You're never feeling your circumstances. You're always feeling your thinking, which, independent of your circumstances, is constantly in a state of flux. This explains why a circumstance can look troubling one moment and okay the next. Knowing that your feelings come from the inside (your thinking), and not the outside (your circumstances), is what allows your state of mind to self-correct when you are troubled." –

Garret Kramer, Sports Psychologist.

When you allow life to be what it is without attaching a narrative to it, suffering is diminished because you cease to oppose what is.
As meaning makers we do it without knowing. We make meanings and compare these meanings to beliefs that are deeply ingrained in our souls. Age old customs of what we should get in certain situations suddenly seem not to line up with the current meanings we are making, and we become terrified. The day of liberation will come when you realize that the belief that is not in tandem with

your current situation was put there by you; and if it was put there by you, you can remove or amend it. In a world of rational thinking, this is just bread, but in **BEING HUMAN** we all fail. As an engineer, I know when to impose constraints on a design and I also know when to remove these constraints or boundaries. If I am doing an analysis where the constraints will not serve my purpose, I remove them, even if for the purpose of the analysis. Once you realize that a belief is not serving your **HAPPINESS**, you can remove it. Although it is sometimes difficult when you are **HUMAN** to know what is going on, you can at the end of every day or week or month or when the occasion demands **PROCESS LIFE.**

We all know how we process orders or how a computer processes information. As occasion demands and at the end of a stressful day, take some time to process the events of the day and how you interpreted them. With this new toolkit, **STEP OUT OF YOURSELF** and process the day. As you do it repeatedly you will begin to see that you are catching yourself more frequently in previous acts that were damaging your mental health. Your mental health begins to heal, and you will begin to be more present in your life and begin experiencing a more fulfilling life.

In Romans 14, Paul begins to explain to the Romans why it is inappropriate to pass judgements on one about certain conducts. *"One person **BELIEVES** that eating vegetables is good but gets stressed out when he sees his brother eating meat, because he believes that eating meat is bad. Another **BELIEVES** that Monday is superior to Saturday and so on.*

Then he gets to verse 14 and says *I am convinced......... that nothing is unclean of itself, except what thinking makes it."*

The reason there is a panel of judges in a subjective competition like a beauty contest is that each of the judges is comparing what they see with what they believe to be beauty. So, at the end of the competition, the contestant with the highest number of judges with **INTERNAL** beliefs agreeing with what they are seeing becomes the winner. Otherwise, all the contestants were *NEUTRALLY EQUALLY BEAUTIFUL* until we brought the ruler of our beliefs into play.

Chapter Six

Life is a Roller Coaster of Thoughts

> *Happiness must happen, and the
> same holds for success:
> you have to let it happen by
> not caring about it".*
> **Viktor E. Frankl**

The other day in a resiliency retreat training session where I and my wife were students in London, a lady who had come to the training from Israel screamed at the facilitator saying,

"All I have learnt in the last two days is that we experience life from our thoughts and not from the external environment, so what else?"

I could see the obvious frustration in her eyes. This is not the first time I will witness such expression of anger. In 2015, I was in a similar training in New Jersey, **USA** when two ladies expressed similar frustration. If you have read the previous chapters and you have similar frustrations, I want to slow down the speed at which we are going a little bit. My first desire is that you really understand what we mean when we say that we experience life from the inside out and not from the outside in. If you do, the implications cover the length and breadth of everything about your life.

In my own life, shortly after my first understanding of what this new paradigm is all about in 2014, I expected all the psychological problems I have had with unwelcomed thoughts to just cease. When this will not happen, I decided to travel for more intense training. I asked one of the facilitators in the New Jersey training, Dr Keith Blevens, why I have not been able to stop unwanted thoughts. He smiled and simply replied, "When we found out about gravity, did we try to stop it?" I could not exactly get where he was going to, but he went further to explain that the purpose of the understanding isn't to stop negative or unwelcomed thoughts; when you understand how life works you are less frightened by life. Once we understood gravity, we stopped asking why objects dropped to the ground.

I remember reading about Michael Neil and how after attending a positive thinking training course, he still could not steady his thoughts or eliminate negative thinking. Another effort at taking a 3-day course on NLP left him nearly depressed until he stumbled into the inside out understanding of how we experience life. Today, Michael Neil is one of the leading teachers of the inside out understanding of life and has written 3 books on the subject – A) – The Inside Out Revolution B) Creating the Impossible and C) The Space Within. I wholeheartedly recommend all three books to those who wish to really explore the inside out understanding of life and how our moment by moment experience of life is created. I have been privileged to sit under Michael Neil in a training session hosted by the three principles UK, a non-profit organization dedicated to promoting the inside out understanding of life.

What I and others who are students of this understanding have learnt is that you cannot control your thoughts all the time. Thoughts come unannounced, whether you are rich or poor whether you are black or white. Scientists say we think over 60000 thoughts per day. If I were to ask you to write down the last 12 thoughts you had before or while reading this book, I bet that you cannot remember them. Your mind is like the clear blue sky above with birds hovering in it and having fun. What distinguishes those with this understanding from those who do not have this understanding is that those who do not have this understanding are terrified when they think negative thoughts.

99% of people who are in psychiatric hospital will be out of the hospital once they understand this paradigm. Just as the thoughts come, they will go. Just let the birds fly, don't try to catch them Once you try to catch them you will get screwed. A very insightful book on this subject is the book **DO NOTHING** by **Damian Mark Smyth**. I first read this book in 2014. It is an amazing book. There is nothing to do when negative thoughts bump into your mind. Just recognize them and go on to do what you planned to do for the day. I did not say resist them; when you resist them, you legitimize them. Just go do what you need to do.

Talking about negative thoughts that just come into your thinking, the late Dr. Kenneth E Hagin says he cannot do anything about it, but he will not give them power or in his words *"he will not let the birds build a nest over his head"*. No teaching will stop you from having occasional, unplanned negative thoughts come into your mind, but once you know that these thoughts are not you and have no life of themselves to harm you (unless you permit them), you will go on to live your life. Unless you are dead, you will have a roller coaster experience of thoughts, but don't give them life. Recognize thought for what it is and go do what you set out to do – you will find the thoughts disappear just as they came. The error that most people make is that they sit down and begin to ponder on these negative thoughts and as they do, they begin to experience their thinking.

Matthew 6: 31. Therefore take no thought, saying, what shall we eat? or, what shall we drink? or, wherewithal shall we be clothed? What was Jesus saying here? The thought "What shall we eat or drink or be clothed" will come; but do not take it. How do you take it? You take it by saying it. In saying it, you give it life. But if you recognize the thought as not yours and go about your day, the thought will disappear just as it came.

 Let me say here that Thoughts and your Thinking are two separate experiences. They are not the same. When people fall into the error of dwelling on the thoughts that flow into their minds, they fall into an error that many people are suffering from today – they go see a psychiatrist. If the psychiatrist is one that does not know how the experience of life is formed, he/she will give them a **LABEL**. Once the psychiatrist gives you a **LABEL**, you are **hooked**!

Let's say the psychiatrist tells you that you are clinically depressed, you go home and start thinking about depression, doing all the Google searches on what depression means and beginning to do a mental construct of a depressed person. You swim in it. You go about telling everyone you see that you are depressed. Once you start thinking the depressive thoughts and the label put on you, you will immediately start feeling the thought. Remember that 100% of our feelings come from our thinking not any event on the outside. The Psychiatrist, Dr Bill Pettit talks about a controlled experiment where the sample children were asked to think 3 negative thoughts, they have had in the past that frightened them. As soon as they started thinking the thoughts, they disrupted the biochemical regulation in their brains within three minutes of the thinking.

Today there are so many people doing trainings on Mental Health who are consigning people to mental illness – people who are perfectly sane but end up insane after wearing a label from a psychiatrist or counsellor. To quote Dr Bill Pettit,

"I am ashamed to say that many mental health practitioners today are actually mental illness practitioners"

Dr Bill Pettit goes on to recommend Stanford University Professor Robert Sapolsky's book **"Why Zebras Don't Get Ulcers"** to show the role that thoughts play in medical depression. I might only recommend this book for medical practitioners as the language seems a bit too advanced for the non-biological/medical mind.

Chapter Seven

Seduced by Consciousness

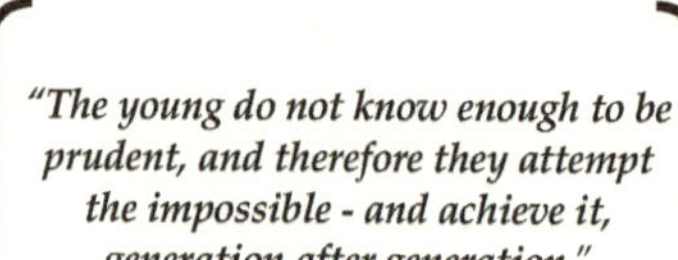

> *"The young do not know enough to be prudent, and therefore they attempt the impossible - and achieve it, generation after generation."*
> - Pearl S. Buck

I was on a flight from London to Lagos in October 2016 after a very disappointing financial performance that year. I started thinking about my age and all the usual meaning making that our minds create. I said to myself that I was past 50 years and it will be getting increasingly difficult to start a new venture or get hired by anybody. Halfway through the six-hour flight, I started thinking about all that I knew about how our life experience is created and how that I am the one making up this seeming logical arguments. I started questioning the reality of these information, wondering where I got them from and why I should start preparing for the end of my career. It dawned on me that I was being influenced by what I gathered from the external environment and what I saw all around me over the years. The thought hit me, what will I do if I was the first man created and have never seen anyone die? What will my thoughts be if I didn't know that people retire at 60 or 70?

I thought to myself, who knows, I might just live forever or maybe live till I was a thousand years and become tired. But even then, because I have never seen anyone tired I might not even be tired.

I wondered if this could be the reason Adam and all the people mentioned in Genesis lived up to 900 years? They had no imagination of anyone dying, didn't know what that meant. It hit me that I was acting on wrong information and that I wasn't true to my creator. I should stop planning my life based on the experience of others.

You see, consciousness is a big issue in our everyday life. Once you become conscious of something, it begins to influence your internal dialogue. Somebody did something and see what happened to him or her that is what is going to happen to me.

However, in truth, your thoughts are not reality. Do not hold on to them if they don't mirror the outcome you desire and expect the same result that others got.

As far back as I can remember, as a student in the University of Benin in the eighties and member of the Christian union, I always was amazed at people coming out to be prayed for, for what did not apply to them. I didn't know what I know now, but I read a lot on psychology and could not see myself come out for most of the prayers, not even when I was under threat. I have a brother who, till this day, thinks that I am very stubborn because I have refused to believe in certain "demon chasing prayers". Whenever he is thinking of assembling an army of prayer warriors to fight the devil, he will always say, "count Tunde out, he doesn't believe in this and will not participate", and I never did.

As a Civil Engineering Student, I knew from simple mechanics that action and reaction must be equal for a body to be in equilibrium.

Also all bodies, experiences and situations will naturally pull towards equilibrium. If you told me to come out to be prayed for not to fail an exam, I must first create the object we want to attack, "the failure". My challenge was that I did not even want to create the object of the fight, so it is useless asking for prayers for something that does not exist. Today, especially in Africa, the job of so called "solution pastors and witch doctors" is booming because there is gross ignorance. People do not know what they are doing.

A lot of persons are in prisons that they built today with the power of ignorance. I have seen young unmarried girls go to "solution pastors and babalawos" to pray against barrenness. To pray against barrenness, when they are not even married? You must first create the barrenness to have something to fight. I remember being in a church service and the pastor narrated a story of how he helped his wife to change her imagination before marriage. Friends and relatives including her senior brother who was yet to have a child after 15 years of marriage have surrounded this lady. She was daily tormented by the thought of not giving birth to children.

This pastor, then her "husband to be" said to her, "Look Linda, you have to fight to stop me from making you have over a dozen kids. I was told that my fertility is so strong that I could impregnate a woman who was 3 months pregnant with another child. So, I am telling you upfront so that you will take the necessary steps to prevent me from giving you a football field of kids. The pastor said this to the "wife to be" every day until marriage and after marriage and exactly nine months after their wedding, they had their first son. Today the couple have 4 kids. You see, the pastor said to the wife, this isn't something to pray about. If the pastor had chosen to fight the imagined fear of bareness, that would have been the beginning of big trouble. Many people innocently lock themselves in prisons built by the consciousness of their environment.

My friend Edith, who is not a medical doctor once shared with me an interesting insight from books she had read and was putting to practice; she said she avoids taking unnecessary drugs as much as is practicable to avoid creating the illness the drug was meant to solve. She said if you administered a drug to a patient for an illness the patient did not have, the body has to look for a way to create the sickness, so the drug will get something to fight. This is taking us back to the equilibrium we talked about earlier on. You see, I am not a medical practitioner to say if she is right or wrong, but the philosophy is mind blowing.

As humans we are seduced by consciousness but we can rise against the reality that consciousness is trying to build in our minds. We can take a deliberate choice to reject consciousness and fall back to our innate wisdom.

Do single unmarried girls surround you and are you already imagining that you may become like one? What is surrounding you is not your reality. You are a meaning maker; choose the meaning you want to make. If the force of the environment is too powerful for you to deal with, you can look for a new environment. This is the reason it is important in your life to choose who you hang out with in life. If all your friends are failing exams, consider making friendship with the people that are taking the first position. You will begin to see that they are people just like you and your imagination will begin to change. Suddenly you will start thinking that you too can make it.

If everyone around you is unemployed, it is time to get new friends that are employed. If everyone around you is talking ill about the company boss and it is affecting your ability to see the company or boss in positive light, then it is time to make new friends in the company who talk well about the company. Think of where you are today and think of any areas that your consciousness has helped to create a meaning that you do not want for your life and start dealing a blow to the consciousness that created that meaning.

It might even be movies that you watched or books that you read. As long as I can remember, possibly as a teenager, I have read biographies that propelled my mind to think of doing the impossible. I have stayed out of movies that frightened me or made me afraid. To this day, I block all whatsapp numbers that send me graphic images that are not helpful for my mental sanity. I do not tolerate videos or images that abuse my mental sanity.

Back to the quote by Pearl S Buck

"The young do not know enough to be prudent, and therefore they attempt the impossible - and achieve it, generation after generation."
The young have no consciousness of limitations and they go on to attempt the impossible. Listen to Paul the Apostle in Romans 7:7 "…For I would not have been conscious of coveting if the law has not said thou shall not covet". EW Kenyon has something beautiful to say about the perils of **SIN CONCIOUSNESS**. I advise you reader to study it.

Chapter Eight

Seduced by Consciousness – 2

We have been to the moon, we have charted the depths of the ocean and the heart of the atom, but we have a fear of looking inward to ourselves because we sense that is where all the contradictions flow together."
Terence McKenna

Why do we go into new relationships, change jobs, change locations etc? The reasons I know could be many and varied: from promotions, changes in family situations etc. I want to dwell on one of the reasons we also sometimes change jobs/relationships – **CONSCIOUSNESS.**

Several years ago, I think this was 1998, I was having serious problems with my marriage. One morning, my wife just left the house with our two kids – (We do have 4 kids now and thank God, a really good marriage now). I was left in an empty house all by myself. My elder brother came visiting with two friends of his, two easy-going fellows that really enjoy drinking. As they tried to cheer me up, my brother's friend Dolapo said humorously *"I hope you are not thinking of divorce and re-marriage? You know I am now in my second marriage and I can tell you from personal experience that all women are the same. I look back and I wonder why I divorced my first wife, she is a lot better than the present one, but I cannot take back the hand of the clock. I sometimes miss my first wife and in comparison, this one is just like a devil".*

If all women or men are the same, why do we then change wives and husbands – (I am not by any means saying that all marriages are 100% alike, there are peculiar challenges in marriages not covered by our discussion on consciousness by which reason, persons might divorce or separate). We opt to divorce and re-marry because we know too much about our spouses. We have made so much internal meanings from their conduct that we have taken those meanings to be reality. Even learning how life is created barely scratches the surface of the reality that we are convinced of.

So, what do we opt for? We want a new spouse that we have no negative internal memory of. We see this new dude, and everything just looks like love on the Caribbean Island. We feel like a "Mills and Boom" new romance novel is about to be written about this seeming new acquaintance. The new person is so perfect and full of everything we desire. If we continue in the delusion we will go with the bliss, divorce this one and marry the new love.

Why do we fall for this seduction? Personal Development is **HARD**. It is very hard I must confess. I have been teaching Personal Development classes for over ten years in companies and I can tell you it is **HARD**. To turn to our thoughts is not the easiest thing to do. The easy thing to do is to place the blame on another. Someone with a grounded understanding of living life from the inside out will say wait a minute, the experience I am having is the product of my thinking not my spouse's behaviour. He or she will begin to explore ways of not letting his/her thoughts hold sway. Read what the wisest man in the Bible had to say about personal development **"He that has rule over his spirit is greater than he that taketh a city" – Proverbs 16:32.** We want to do great things, but the last thing we want to do is look inside ourselves.

My brother's friend's experience is quite instructive. The "other flame" may just not be different from the one at home. Soon, differences in realities will creep up and arguments will start. As it is, all arguments stem from a failure to recognize the principle of separate realities. As the arguments come up, new meanings are created every day. As the brain creates these meanings, it automatically compares them to meanings made about the previous relationships. If you have taken any course on computer programming, you will remember the "IF" command. If this is greater than that "assign zero", if less "assign null". So, your **AI** algorithm quickly starts creating new rules of engagement as meanings emerge in the relationship.

Take a glass of heavily disturbed mud water and just leave it to settle. After a while, you will see clear sparkling water with all sediments buried at the bottom of the glass. When we are in a difficult quarrel or disagreement of any kind, we are like that glass of mud water, severely disturbed in our thoughts. We lose **CLARITY** and currently many of the decisions we make are based on this wrong judgement. What this understanding helps us to do is that if we will just **do nothing** and wait for the disturbing thoughts to clear, we will return to our natural state of wisdom and see things differently. Many of us reading this article might have read the admonition *"do not make important decisions of your life when you are angry, stressed, troubled, bitter, in anguish of soul or in the middle of a fierce disagreement".*

I will tell you the truth, the bitter lesson is that this is the time 90% of people want to make the most important decision of their lives. We are so convinced that this muddled mud water is the permanent reality of our lives and that the mud will never settle. Is it any wonder the pain we all go through in our lives?

Imagine the challenge of the trick your brain is playing on you in a new relationship. Now you are in a new relationship, the mud in the old relationship has settled and you do not feel the same way you felt again when the arguments were in their peak. Meanwhile in the new relationship, turbulence is at its peak. What do many couples do? You sneak back to the old relationship and possibly start a secret affair or a full-blown relationship. I have counselled a few people who are about changing jobs. In many of the stories, I can see that a relationship has gone sour in their place of work. I can see that they have made a dictionary full of negative meanings that they are even ready to quit without a new job. I have been a victim myself in many botched jobs. I just wanted to jump into the sea and forget I ever worked in the company. Then the new job comes, and I run to give testimony in church. I have barely enjoyed my new testimony before the principle of separate realities kicks in. I can now barely agree with the man who was interviewing me yesterday that looked like an angel. My **AI** starts telling me the old boss is better than this new one.

Before long, I start calling my old boss that I swore **NEVER** to contact again. I call him because I want to keep the door open for a return from exile. I remember one painful exit that happened. This job was one of the best jobs I ever got, the pecks of the job were just amazing. Without any new job and 4 kids in private schools, I resigned. Boy, did I go hungry? I threw the entire family into a big mess. I lived in a company accommodation, had company car, company driver, even though I was living in Nigeria, I was paid in US dollars. I had to give up every company entitlement. If I had the understanding I have now, I might not have quit the way I did. My thoughts got me screwed.

In counselling people who want to leave their employment today, I show them the power of thought and their responsibility in the understanding of how life works. I let them see our roles as meaning makers and tell them if you **FULLY** understand what I am saying, you can make your choice. If you think that the meanings in your computer's hard drive cannot be erased, then it might be safe to try a new job; but first take some time off work, if you have outstanding leave, take the leave and let your natural wisdom or calmness return to you. If possible, take an unpaid job during your leave to see what other organizational cultures teach you. If in your calmness you still feel persuaded that the right thing to do is to resign, then resign. My advice in any form of relationship will not differ much except that in a marriage relationship where the stakes are much more, you may want to triple the exercise above, seek out counsel and really make a decision that is from your God given wisdom.

I love a phrase I come across often in the bible. "Adam **KNEW** his wife…" It connotes **CONSCIOUSNESS**! The word **KNEW** carries a lot of meaning. Once I "**KNEW**" you, the mystery about you is gone. Until I "**KNEW**" you, you were just a beautiful garden. When I came near, the grasses weren't as beautiful as I thought a mile away. In 2 Sam13, David's son desperately lusted after his sister Tamar. Immediately after he "**KNEW**" her he hated her terribly. He was screwed by consciousness.

Understanding how life works won't stop you from changing jobs or relationships etc. This time, you will make any decision from a deeper place within you, not just your emotional transient feelings.

Chapter Nine

Seduced by Consciousness -3

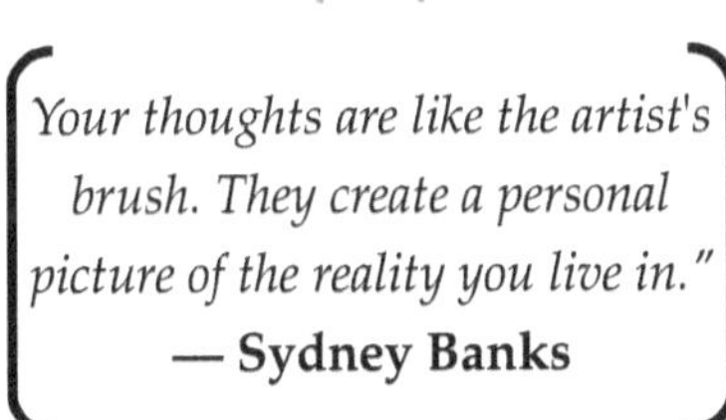

Your thoughts are like the artist's brush. They create a personal picture of the reality you live in."
— **Sydney Banks**

In one of several stories in his book "Seduced by Consciousness", Jack Pransky tells an experience in Japan about a time a Tsunami was to happen. As people suspected that electricity will be cut off for a season, many flocked to the supermarket to buy foods like "granola" that did not require electric cooking or preservation. When he got to the Supermarket, the checkout queue was spilling out into the streets. He entered the supermarket expecting that he will spend so long in the supermarket as he was preparing to pick up his "granolas" and join the queue. Somehow instead of coming out to join the queue of people queuing unto the streets he decided to just wonder deep into a different section of the supermarket. To his amazement, he saw a check out till with no customer at the end of the supermarket. He just went to the till operator, paid and came out through the entrance with people queuing unto the streets.

Many things in our lives are like this experience. Once we read a story, we are frightened with the thought that this too will happen to us. We are blind to other possibilities that could exist in the circumstance. We do not even try any more. Our consciousness has placed a limitation on our ability to explore other options. Guess what? The tsunami did not occur as forecasted. There was no destruction.

What does it mean to be seduced by consciousness? To take an awareness that you have about an issue and make it your own reality. The purpose of this chapter is to see how we can avoid the subtle suggestions of seductive thoughts that work against us. It is not a bad thing to be seduced, but we want to be seduced with something that we desire, not what we do not desire. One impact of hanging out with the right crowd is that you get seduced by the community energy generated by the company. If you walk with wise people, their wisdom will rub off on you, if you work with foolish people, their foolishness will equally rub off on you.

Several years ago, I went into business for myself and things became really tough. Gradually, rather than think my way out of the mess, my friends who were equally running similar entrepreneurial ventures started converging in my small office to talk about the then Nigerian president and how his leadership was hindering us all from succeeding. They say, "Birds of the same feather flock together", so it did not take time for friends with struggling start-up businesses to gather at my office every morning to complain. One of the reasons they converged in my office was that I was the only person in the bunch that could afford a newspaper every morning. Prior to this association I would spend my idle moments reading books that will keep my hope alive.

Gradually, this association of unproductive entrepreneurs grew and grew, and we were saying highfalutin words like we will take over the government, we will organize a coup and on and on. It was so real in my thoughts that all Nigerians were going through what we were going through. I have gradually forgotten the inspiring stories of hope that I read which kept me alive.

One day, I could not make the daily idle meetings; I stayed at home and re-read one of my inspiring motivational books again. My eyes opened. What am I doing with these bunch and all these idle talks of overthrowing a military head of state. How in the world did I come to think that everyone is going through what I am going through? People are working.

Some businesses are collapsing while some are increasing in leaps and bounds. I have a choice, to either close the business and go look for a job or put life into the business, but to sit and just chatter away my time did not do me any good. Besides who told me that a bunch of around seven unemployed young adults can overthrow a military head of state? As I thought about the time I had lost in these unproductive meetings, I was very angry with myself.

Idle foolish talk will just deepen my misery. I do not even have enough money to pay my transport to Abuja (the seat of Government) let alone buy a bullet. If I was the most financially liquid of the bunch, you can imagine that none of the naysayers can afford a bus fare to Abuja either. It was just idle talk that helped us get seduced to think that everyone else was idle. If the police was to arrest us for idle foolish talk, I bet that none of us had money to get bail. You see in every economy, people are working. Even in economies where unemployment is 50%, it means 50% of the population are working. You can choose to associate with the consciousness of those working and become eventually employed yourself or with the 50% nay Sayers and remain there and think that everyone is there with you.

Even today, many of us remain deluded by the consciousness of "nothing is working", but the likes of Dangote, Jim Ovia, Tony Elumelu and several thousands of their type are working every day and increasing their market share. Several businesses are thriving, and people are getting hired every day. The other day I met a young man in a restaurant in Akure and he told me had no job; when I asked him what he studied and the firms to which he had made job applications, he said there was no need as there are no jobs. I said to him, you are seduced by the wrong consciousness. People are getting hired every day, others are leaving the country and getting lucrative jobs abroad, you can't sit at home and expect that the job will drop from the sky; not with this kind of seduction.

Back to my story with my deluded friends. I made up my mind that from the next morning, my office will cease to be a meeting point for aimless talk. I got to my office the next morning and put a small paper at the front of the door saying that "visitors are only welcome from 6pm", once I entered the office, I locked myself inside. Of course, by 6pm the office will be closed. Were my friends angry with me? They were very angry and some vowed never to talk to me again. Did it bother me? Not at all. I have always believed that you cannot argue with results. It didn't take long I was back to my reading and meditation practices; my business improved and within a year I made my first business trip to the United States, spent 11 days in the US and returned to Nigeria. Those angry friends came back wanting to find out what I was doing differently. By the books I read, I had changed my consciousness – I have become seduced by a new kind of consciousness.

Today, many are stuck on social media meditating on every evil video that speaks of Armageddon getting so close. I am sorry but your experience is a self-created reality. Armageddon isn't coming tomorrow, we are commissioning Dangote refinery tomorrow not waiting for an Armageddon. Get books that inspire, associate with people that elevate your consciousness, take deliberate steps to improve your life. Solomon said in the Bible, "The sluggard said there is a lion (unemployment) in the way and refused to go out". But he called him a sluggard because he was seduced with a wrong consciousness. There was no lion anywhere. Others went to work and passed the very same route, they sent speculative CVs to companies with even no vacancies and were hired.

In the course of some of my public speaking engagement today, I have come across young energetic graduates who are wasting the very best energy of their lives. They are criticizing everything, from Buhari to Donald Trump. I found myself to be very angry with Donald Trump recently; but I said softly to myself, that this anger is just **created by my THOUGHTS**. Donald Trump is in the white house, I am in Ajah with no electricity; my anger has nothing to do with his work. I am not even a US citizen. Trump is attending to his business; I too should attend to my business. I can make better use of my thoughts than generate a whole lot of negative energy that does me no good.

It may be very tough for you today, I know; I have been there, I have been in "the valley of death" a few times, it could be **HOPELESS**, but don't make yourself more hopeless. A change in consciousness is the first thing that will take you out of that valley of hopelessness. Sometimes, it doesn't cost any money to make a change. For some, it may just be reducing time spent on social media from eight hours to 2hours per day and spending the rest of this wasted time reading books that build hope and courage. For others, it just may mean changing your current abode and for the rest changing the crowd that you hang out with. Armageddon or a holiday in the Caribbean is just a thought creation that can be done by choosing what you want to be seduced with. I wish you a positive seduction of consciousness.

Chapter Ten

Dealing with Seductive Thoughts

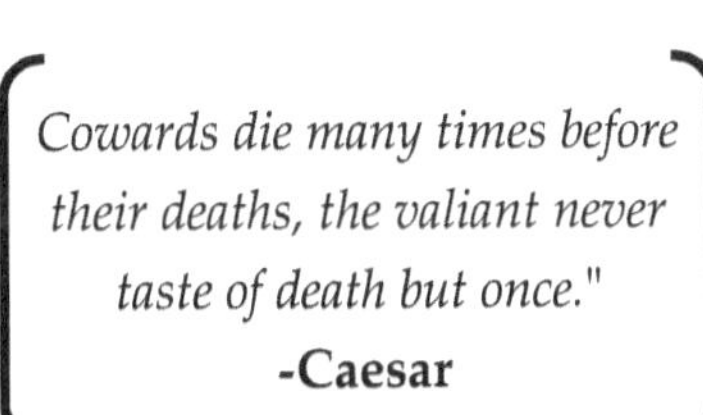

Cowards die many times before their deaths, the valiant never taste of death but once."
-Caesar

Caesar's wife, Calpurnia, has had dreams in which her husband was murdered. At Caesar's request, the priests have sacrificed an animal which, upon being cut open, was discovered to have no heart. And so, they sent word to Caesar that he should stay home on this fateful day, the ides of March, which the Soothsayer had already warned him about earlier in the play.
Caesar muses,"
"What can be avoided / whose end is purposed by the mighty gods?"

In other words, if the gods are predicting that he is going to die, then how will he get around it? He goes on to encourage his wife with the now-famous lines, finding it strange that men fear death so much, when death is inevitable in every man's life. He has been a strong and brave man and has not wasted precious hours of his life anticipating tragedy.

Unwanted thoughts, unwanted dreams, horrifying images/videos, movies, past mistakes, past abuses, false prophesies, past failures, past losses, past relationship failures are just some of the fears that haunt and torment us in our everyday lives. I have myself been a victim in several areas of my life. Several years ago, I started a taxi business with two other friends. After six months of turmoil and massive losses, the business closed shop. My subconscious Artificial Intelligence warned me never to get involved with anything related to taxi business again. Five years down the line, my in-law comes to me for advice; I told him that taxi business was a money sucking business.

I was wrong; there are several millionaires today who run a taxi business. In case, you don't know, UBER is a taxi company. You see, many of the advice that the aged give the young ones today are dead WRONG. I believe with all my heart that kids and young adults should be taught to walk on the moon before they are 25. Many of us adults unaware of the role of consciousness give very limiting advice. It was my realization of this concept that led me to begin my work with indigent kids – to set their minds on fire before consciousness places limitation on them. Remember the quote by *Pearl S Buck?*

"The young do not know enough to be prudent, and therefore they attempt the impossible – and achieve it, generation after generation."

If you are a young man/woman today reading this book, I am challenging you not to settle for anything other than the "moon". Let no day go by without you increasing the fire of the passion burning in you. Forget about limitations, limitations are the product of consciousness.

I remember listening to *John H Johnson*, publisher of *Ebony Magazine* and for much of his life the richest African American in the United States. He started his business with a $500-dollar loan secured by his mother's furniture. The $500 loan was to print the first edition of the "Negro Digest". There was no contingency in case the magazine did not sell. He said in his autobiography that if the first "Negro Digest" did not sell, that would have been the end of the Johnson Publishing Company. Later, when he had become a multimillionaire and read business plans from Harvard Business School, he came to know that the way he started business was wrong. Harvard MBA showed him that he should have had contingency plans for every eventuality.

He confessed in his autobiography that if he knew what he would later learn from **MBA**, he would never have attempted Johnson Publishing. He *did not know* it was possible for the magazine not to sell. His plan to his mother was simple; I will make the first print with the $500 and from the sales I will make $500 profit and print the next one and on and on. John H Johnson went on to give the same advice that many **CONSCIOUS** adults give young people today. He said in his book that he will not advise anyone to go into business today the way he did, even though he went on to define success as **Hard work + IGNORANCE.**

In my own little life, I decided in 2003 to go pursue an MBA in the Republic of Ireland. All the preparation was a savings of one thousand euros for the admission acceptance fees and a small article I read that describes how you can bungle your way through graduate studies by working part time. Immediately I got the admission, I sold the few properties I owned in my rented flat in Lagos, my car, my wife's car, and everything to bathroom sandals. I took a one-way flight with less than a thousand euros to take care of a wife and 4 kids. The story is a long one for another day, but like John H Johnson, I completed my MBA in 2004, got a job and worked in Europe for several years as General Manager of a medium sized manufacturing company. Years later, a friend in Port Harcourt, with wife and 3 kids wanted to do the same thing and came to me for advice. I told him not to try it. Why will I give that kind of advice when on every count, my adventure was a huge success? Like John H Johnson, I have become conscious of the challenges of what I did **AFTER** I did it. My advice to my friend was wrong. I know better now, and I should be able to give better counsel next time. I was seduced by the wrong consciousness.

Caesar's wife had a dream of Caesar being murdered. What should she do? This is an interesting experience that traumatizes many. This week, a fellow in Delta State, Nigeria, travelling from Akwa Ibom to Warri sent me this comment after reading *"Seduced by consciousness -3"*.

"Thank you for the above inspiring write up. 60 percent of the above happened to me yesterday. While travelling at that odd hour yesterday, so many scary thoughts that I have read up and seen on social media came to my mind, the young girls that I read that had fallen victim in the same situation I was in yesterday. I became scared that I wanted to spend a night in a stranger's house (I wonder what would have been my story by now) because of other people's stories. Controlling one's consciousness is a difficult task. I tried to shift my mind from my fears but this will not happen. What else could I have done in the situation?"

About a year ago after I started learning how life is internally self-created, a lady who was having severe work challenges approached me for advice. I quietly listened to her for over an hour and asked a few questions. During the conversation, I tried to show her the role that our thoughts play in "suspecting or imagining the worst to happen" to her. She told me she understood perfectly what I was trying to say, but then she asked me "what if there is really a plan to sack her like they did to another colleague?" She was suspecting that she was being set up by her superiors for termination. Here was my answer; "if you believe that they are planning against you, you will start acting to counter the plan, or at least with the knowledge that you are dealing with enemies not friends; but if you train yourself to believe that you are the one making up the thoughts, you will have a more harmonious relationship with them. I went on to say that if they were planning to sack you 30 days from now, if you believe it was you making this meaning, you will taste the sack once, but if you believe that they are planning to sack you for real, you will experience the sack every day. I asked her, "Which of them do you want?" She said she preferred to experience the sack once. It is over one year now since this conversation took place, she is not only working in the same organization but has been promoted. You see "Cowards die many times before their deaths, the valiant never taste of death but once."

The Bible says Love Believes the best of everyone, not the worst. The book of Hebrews says men's hearts are failing them for "Fear of the things……" **NOT the things**, but the Fear of. What is that image or thought that is trying to stifle life out of you? You can regain your life by **CHOOSING** what to believe and by believing the **BEST.**

We will look at Caesar's wife's dream and Youth Corps Member's story in the next chapter

Chapter Eleven

Dealing with Seductive Thoughts -2

> *"If you have built castles in*
> *the air, your work need not*
> *be lost; that is where they should be.*
> *Now put the foundations under them".*
> *-Henry David Thoreau*

No matter how we try we can never eliminate all unwanted thoughts from flying over our heads. Whether it is the dream from Caesar's wife, or the lady who was travelling in the thick of the night, or the person who was besieged by a past relationship failure, some of these thoughts or imaginations just show up. As I was reflecting on my admonition to young people to learn how to walk on the moon before over consciousness sets in, I remembered a message my friend, Rev John Emilimor, sent to me some years ago; in the message, Rev John quoted Henry David Thoreau **"If you have built castles in the air, your work need not be lost; that is where they should be. Now put the foundations under them".** I quite enjoyed the admonition then and for me this is especially advised for young people; **BUILD YOUR LIFE BEFORE ACQUIRING CONSCIOUSNESS OF THE AGED.**

The quote is from Henry David Thoreau's book **Walden,** and the specific paragraph reads *"I learned this, at least, by my experiment: that* *if one advances confidently in the direction of his dreams, and endeavours to live the life which he has imagined, he will meet with a success unexpected in common hours. He will put some things behind, **will pass an invisible boundary; new, universal, and more liberal laws will begin to establish themselves around and within him; or the old laws be expanded, and interpreted in his favour** in a more liberal sense, and he **will live with the license of a higher order of beings**. In proportion as he simplifies his life, the laws of the universe will appear less complex, and solitude will not be solitude, nor poverty, poverty, nor weakness, weakness. If you have built castles in the air, your work need not be lost; that is where they should be. Now put the foundations under them."*

What will you do if you were Calpurnia, Caesar's wife after a terrible dream? Some of us have had terrible dreams in the night and awaken to the reality that it was just a dream. For some others it is not just a dream, it is a so-called prophecy. Some years ago, I was attending a church where prophecies were rampant; many of the prophesies were quite scary, others quite manipulative.

Somehow, the prophets feared manipulating me. I confided in a friend that there was **ONLY** one prophecy that I would **<u>ACCEPT</u>** – (You see, you have to accept a prophecy, good or bad for it to have any power in your life), and that was the prophecy that will say **"TUNDE, YOU WILL BE PRESIDENT OF NIGERIA"**. I was about 22 years old at this time, but I was quite read. You really need to eat well to manipulate me by fear.

I saw people who were miserable because one of the so-called prophets predicted a future they did not desire. To get at me, these prophets tried to seduce me. They prophesied what will suit my ego from time to time and one day, they took the sledge hammer and prophesied that I was going to be married to a certain girl in the church; a girl (**I NEVER LIKED NOR HAD ANY FEELINGS FOR**) and if I didn't marry her God will kill me. After weeks of ego boosting prophesies, they got me. I got seduced for a while and then met a friend who was as studious as me in spiritual things. We reasoned together and dismissed the evil prophecy and I walked away from that church. Are you seduced by prophecy? You can untangle yourself from that bondage, whatever religious organization or native doctor that may have put that spell on you.

As an African, Shakespeare's writings are quite instructive; it tells me that everyone is aware of some life/existence beyond the senses. Africans are quite fetish. What will you do as Caesar if after your wife's dream, you order the priest to make a sacrifice and when the animal is sacrificed, there was **NO HEART**. Caesar, like some of us, was in between fear and courage. He tells the wife Calpurnia that "cowards die many times before their death, but the valiant never taste death but once". That is quite a courageous statement to make; but then Caesar, vacillating between courage and fear, orders for a sacrifice. Remember part one of seduced by consciousness? To fight something, you must "create it".

Job in the bible is one person who did what Caesar did. He said, "that which I greatly feared has come upon me". The thought will be there, but you have to act on it for it to take over you. Job performed sacrifices every day to deal with the fear. What do you think repeating the same sacrifices everyday will do to his consciousness?

READ SIN CONCIOUSNESS BY EW KENYON. It will make him more conscious of the thing he did not want. Except for some of the things I now know and even at that I must still trust God not to be controlled by fear after seeing an animal sacrificed for my safety with *no heart*.

Let's revisit Caesar's statement "Cowards die many times before their death, but the valiant only taste death but once". You see, to me cowards get a fearful thought and begin to live by the dictates and boundaries of the fear. If death was a predetermined certainty for Caesar, which will be better? To live courageously and die on the "ides of March" or to live so fearfully that your life is not worth living and still die on the "ides of March?". I bet you that I will choose to live courageously and die on the "ides of March" than take in the fear and still die.

Here is a response if I were Caesar receiving that terrible dream from Calpurnia. I may not know exactly what to do **AT THE VERY MOMENT**. You see, our momentary life is different from our logical life. Many times, we are faced with dire situations that require a response from us in milliseconds. A decision tree diagram in these moments is not possible and, in some cases, our ability to think rationally is heavily diminished. But here is where to begin your liberation, **BELIEVE THAT THERE IS A WAY TO FREEDOM** *that you do not know*.

Once that belief is triggered in you, your spirit goes to work. You may not feel any different. You may be submerged in FEAR, but even as you are shaking in dread, just BELIEVE. If you believe there is a way out, you will find the way, if you believe there is no way, you will give up. To recant one of **Jim Rohn**'s quote, *"If you really want to do something you will find a way, if you don't, you will find an excuse"*. Start with believing that this is **NOT** your end. Your emotions may be screaming, but don worry about your emotions, it is normal. Remember the story of Jesus going to the cross? Even with certainty that there is a way out, His sweat was so thick that it came out like blood. Luke 22:44 *"And being in anguish, he prayed more earnestly, and his sweat was like drops of blood falling to the ground"*.

You see, the foundational thrust that gave birth to **Nuclear Physics** was that **THERE IS SUFFICIENT ENERGY IN AN ATOM TO POWER A GREAT SHIP FROM LONDON TO NEW YORK**. Albert Einstein sent a letter of his conviction on this to President Roosevelt on Aug 2, 1939. Today Nuclear power is all history. You see, there is sufficient power in each one of us to liberate us from the most **IMPOSSIBLE SITUATIONS OR PRISONS IN EVERY ONE OF OUR LIVES** and the starting point towards accessing this power is **BELIEF**. Step on the ladder of **BELIEF THAT THERE IS A WAY OUT**. Do not bother about the details on the **HOW**. Just **BELIEVE!** After the **BELIEVE**, tell Calpurnia that you will take her for dinner on March 16. The ides of March is March 15. You must be alive to take her out on March 16. I did not say pray. I say verbalize a plan that goes against the evil haunting you or rather, that affirms what you want. Don't worry, if you are stammering. I will personally stammer, but I know laws that created this universe and I know my part in having them work for me or against me.

Chapter Twelve

Dealing with Seductive Thoughts - Conscious Consciousness

> *If the only thing people learned was not to be afraid of their experience, that alone would change the world."*
> – Sydney Banks

From dreams to movies, none of us is immune from momentary psychological states of fear or helplessness. The American motivational speaker Les Brown narrates what happened to him after watching the horror movie, **"THE EXORCIST"**. For two weeks, he slept with the lights in his room turned on. Is watching horror films bad? Not at all; but again, just follow the admonition by Socrates "Man Know thyself". You should know yourself. Remember the thrust of this book , **ALL PSYCHOLOGICAL LIFE IS INTERNALLY SELF CREATED**. We all create different meanings from what we see. If I am not creating good meanings from what I see, I think I want to see less of it.

We are professional meaning makers. We create our experience of life from the inside not from the outside. Remember Damian Mark Smyth's book **"Do Nothing"**? I think that is one part of the answer to the night traveller who asked how to change her mind from those fearful thoughts. My first answer is do nothing. When you realize that it is consciousness trying to frighten you, you just **do**

NOTHING. If I may ask, is everyone travelling in the car having the same feelings of fear? I can bet you that some in the vehicle are fast asleep. Not everyone in the vehicle have read the same stories as this lady. So why they are sleeping, she is riddled with fear. She is relating with a consciousness that the other passengers don't have.

That is why we say that our experience of life is from the inside and not from the outside. All that is first required of us is just to **RECOGNIZE** that we are the ones making this meaning and our thoughts are not reality. Live the fear and do what you want to do. I have not read **Susan Jeffers** book, but I think I just enjoy the title **"Feel the fear and do it Anyway"**. Many times, we cannot eliminate the feeling of fear. But we can use our understanding of life to feel the fear and be OK. To emphasize the quote above from Sydney Banks, *"If the only thing people learned was not to be afraid of their experience, that alone would change the world."*
"What you feel doesn't matter in the end; it's what you do that makes you brave". -**Andre Agassi**

The American, **Kenneth Copeland** also prescribes the second thing to do after recognition of the source of the fear. In a thought experiment, he asks his listeners to count 1 to 10 in their thinking and while they are doing the counting, he asks them to say their names. According to him, the act of saying your name breaks the act of number counting. He says in the same way, when fearful thoughts are hounding you just say what you know to be true rather than pay attention to the thoughts. In the case of the night traveller, start saying in a muted voice (meditative practice) what you will do when you get to Warri. As you say things like "when I get to Warri I will first eat rice, watch a good movie and take a cold shower….." the weight of the fear will begin to disappear and your consciousness will begin to shift in the moment. Don't try to resist the other Consciousness; your mind will gradually start thinking about what you will do on arrival.

I like what **Dr Judith Sedgeman** has to say on the subject. *"We take in information and then we create our own thoughts about it. We do not act on the information; we act on our own thoughts about it. The direction our thoughts go has a lot to do with our knowledge of what is going on in our minds, and the depth of our own recognition that when the train of thought is leading to anxiety, self-doubt, fear or darkness, we can change direction. The types of thoughts that continue to come to mind are defined by the state of mind in which we are thinking. If we are calm and confident, we'll continue to think of increasingly constructive things. If we are stressed and fearful, we'll think of increasingly less constructive things. If we don't like the feeling state our thinking is leading us through, we can change our minds.*

*There is one and only one reason for thoughts of anxiety breeding thoughts of fear, breeding thoughts of panic, breeding hysteria. That reason is upsetting thoughts **taken increasingly seriously**. For those who understand that their rising levels of tension are being produced by their own thinking, not by events or circumstances, this doesn't happen. They know they have a choice, and one choice is to pause, let the flow of negative thoughts pass and allow their minds to quiet. A whole different quality of thinking will arise from a calmer state of mind".*

Today, the understanding that life is internally self-created is so important. The news media is in frenzy about political happenings. There are many who are interpreting the happenings as meaning that there is trouble ahead. That trouble is just being created by people's thoughts. It is not reality. Once you catch yourself as the *interpreter in chief* of what you read, the information holds less value and meaning. We take in the news about what is going on and we make our internal meanings out of it. There is not one reality about what you read concerning elections.

Everyone makes their own meaning from what they are reading, and no two meanings are the same. Some people are in such states of anger they are prepared for a fight, but if you have read my earlier write up on the *"Principle of Separate Realities"*, there is nothing to fight about. We are all creating our reality from something that has no meaning. I can disagree and be **OK** if someone says **PMB** has performed 100%; I can disagree also and be **OK** if another says his performance is zero percent. It is just separate realities playing out.

My reality doesn't have to be the same as that of my wife for us to live peacefully together. It is just misunderstanding of how life is created that is playing on us. It is not wrong to make your own meaning, it is only wrong if you ignorantly think that your meaning is *the reality.*

Any thought engulfing you today is self-created. We are expert meaning makers, but we are unaware that we are the ones making the meaning. You may be in a marriage today and say "this is the worst spouse in the world"; but the reality check is that you came up with this assertion, that creation of thought is not reality; it is something that you made up.

Conscious Consciousness

We should all challenge ourselves to create the consciousness we want on purpose. Make friends with people who will help you move forward in life; life is challenging enough without any interference, I don't want to add a consciousness that I can avoid. I want to watch movies that keep me refreshed not ones that leave me fearful; I want to read books that make me want to live not those that make me want to die. I want occasions that will help me scream **"LIFE IS GOOD"**.

We cannot always control 100% of the experiences that our thoughts interact with, but within the conscious choices that we make, let's go for what will propel us forward. Every living person in this world has a challenge or what you call problem. If there is anyone without a problem I can bet you that person is a dead man, not a living person. The difference amongst us is that while some consciously focus on the good, the others focus on the problem.

It is a whole lot of difference when you begin to practice simple acts of gratitude. Count your blessings, name them one by one …… Become consciously conscious of the good happening in your life. If you did 10 things today and 9 did not go as you wanted, direct your attention to the only one that worked. What you focus on *expands*. As you focus on what works, your life will be flooded with life. Some persons have 9 things work for them and one yet to unfold and they sabotage their lives focusing on the one that is still unfolding.

American businesswoman, **Mary Kay Ash** says that *"Aerodynamically speaking, the bumblebee shouldn't be able to fly, but the* *bumblebee doesn't know that, so it goes to fly anyway"*. Stop acquiring a consciousness that does not serve your aspirations. Not every information you are seeking for is helpful. Stop looking for negative information about people, and this includes your spouse, relatives, friends etc. Stop looking for statistical information to confirm your fears. Be like the bumblebee, **FLY WHEN EVERYONE THINKS YOU SHOULDN'T**.

Chapter Thirteen

Conscious Parenting

In a sort of ghastly simplicity, we remove the organ and demand the function. We make men without chests and expect of them virtue and enterprise. We laugh at honour and are shocked to find traitors in our midst. We castrate and bid the geldings be fruitful."
— **C.S. Lewis, The Abolition of Man**

In 1993 I decided to attend a one-month Bible Course at the Living Faith Church, in a special program tagged **WOFBI**. I was 26 at the time. The program got me so fired up about the bible; I took everything I learnt hook, line and sinker. Fast track to June 2018, 25 years later, I decided to take the same course again. The content and the mode of delivery remained the same. The effectiveness and the energy of the facilitators were as strong as ever; but this time I did not take everything hook, line and sinker. Why? Consciousness has acted on me along the way. 25 years ago, I was not as conscious as I was today. As the bible school lecturers spoke with so much energy, my mind was all over the place trying to even focus. From worries about bills to pay to awareness of how so and so prayed the same prayer and yet died, I wasn't as fired up like I was in my first study. I even challenged some of what the lecturers taught. As I reflected on the difference between Tunde 1993 and Tunde 2018, I saw the impact of consciousness.

My friend, Rev John Emilimor's son, came to him and asked him why he was still in Chapter 2 (after 2 weeks) of reading a book that he (the son) finished in 4 hours? My friend laughed, he said his son's brain was clear, his was saddled with all the responsibilities of life. He said he read one paragraph for hours because he was distracted by bills that were overdue.

I was discussing with my wife about my experiences in both bible courses and I repeated my admonition that young people should succeed before consciousness. I told her that many of the pastors we label as fake today were as genuine as they can be when they went into pastoral work; but as they executed the office, and like **ALL OF US WHO NOW LOOK FAKE**, we gave heed to too much consciousness of things that did not work the way we expected and began to behave in the manner we label as fake today. I went on to tell my wife that how we internalize and interpret consciousness matters a lot. I said to her that it is difficult for any wealthy person today to be able to act in such a way as to transfer his/her wealth creation ability to their kids because of this wrong interpretation of life.

Many wealthy people today came from the bottom of the pyramid and fought their way to the top of the pyramid. In fighting their way to the top of the pyramid, they endured so much affliction, suffering and pain. When they got to the top of the pyramid, they internally misinterpreted the journey. The suffering, affliction and the pains are what made the journey worthwhile. Man was created for adventure. Have you ever wondered why people will spend $70,000 to climb mount Everest? Remove adventure and life becomes meaningless. If the creator did not plan for us to go through pains and struggles, we should have shown up in this world, fully developed, with modern high-speed trains, aircrafts, computing intelligence etc.

We make wrong meanings of our struggles and work to protect our children from going through what we have gone through. Is it any wonder that these kids grow up behaving abnormally? Nowhere is this more prevalent than developing countries. There is so much pain and fatigue in the process of getting to the top of the pyramid in developing countries that when those who make it get to the top, they work day and night to protect their kids from seeing challenges. Their kids have a retinue of drivers, nannies, carers, they attend elitist schools that ensure they don't even use their brains. The parents even see the exercise of mental ability as bad for them. They get big bank accounts even when they are not working. They are driving cars that they may never be able to buy with their earnings in a lifetime given their poor mental development. The problem isn't just the kids, the real problem is the meanings that their parents made from their own struggles.

CS Lewis in his book, **THE ABOLITION OF MAN** says we remove the organ and yet require them to function and be fruitful. The organ of fruitfulness has long been removed. What we need to do as parents is to re-configure the internal meanings we make of our suffering. Rain, sunshine, heat and cold are all necessary for growth. To protect the plant from any of these is to produce an abnormal plant.

Robert H Schuler built the crystal cathedral. At the time it was built, it was the most elegant church building in the world. Desperate to protect his son from going through pain, he brought him in as pastor of the church. The young man preached every Sunday with a feeling of emptiness. One day, he went to his father and resigned as the pastor of the church. The father was in tears. The son told his father he was going to start his own church in an abandoned building; that made his father more sorrowful for him. His father told him all the challenges he is going to meet, all the heartaches and pains. The father narrated his own pains starting from the bottom of the pyramid to building the crystal cathedral and told him to think again. The young son replied and told the father that those were the exact stories that his heart was yearning for. The son said he wanted to experience real life, to see suffering and how to win in spite of it. The son left the pastorate of crystal cathedral and went on to establish his own church and today has made a mega success of his career.

In my personal life, I tried for years to protect my kids until it dawned on me one day that I was taking away their organ. One of my sons, after SS3 seemed so frightened to go to University. He long wanted me to remove the protection around him, but I feared doing it. He demanded entering public transport instead of being chauffer driven. The first week I gave him the liberty to enter public transportation in Lagos, I was amazed; his whole face lit up; he felt like he was now a man, he came home and hugged me that he was now ready to go to University. I just could not believe what had just happened. You see, man was created for adventure. Your kids will blame you tomorrow if you take away their organ and hunger for adventure.

In the book of numbers, in the Bible, God told the leaders of Israel how to apportion the land. After giving them instructions on how to apportion the land, he told them that some of the territories *with enemies living in it* were for their kids and that the parents <u>*CANNOT*</u> fight the battle reserved for their kids. Today I see wealth changing hands in every generation because many wealthy persons have castrated their children.

I know a man who is my age mate today, when he was young his father protected him from the exercise of his mental capacities; today he works in one of the companies owned by his father's house maid (servant). The father's house boy struggled through public schools, read at odd hours of the night when he was done with house chores and he eventually attended the University of Benin while I was a student there. Immediately after graduation, he joined Chevron and established several businesses in Lagos and today has hired the same person who was sending him on errands as a boy, as a unit manager in one of his establishments.

When parents fight to stop their kids from exercising themselves mentally, they are only increasing the pains the kids will suffer in the future. I will once again repeat my admonition to young people, get to the moon before you know how to get there. You need just a little knowledge to do what you want to do; take action. People who are endlessly searching for how to build a successful business never get started.

People who are endlessly searching for how to have a hitch free marriage never get married. Get a little knowledge, then marry. Remember John H Johnson's formula? Success is **HARDWORK +**

IGNORANCE.

What is over consciousness? Too much awareness of what can go wrong. You don't need all that bunch of information. Go read about every successful business, the people who launched them had just 5% knowledge of what they wanted to do and acted. The critics stayed by the sides analysing all that can possibly go wrong. I remember reading a story where Richard Branson talks about hiring a professor to analyse the opportunities in an idea; after waiting for days for the professor to come up with his submission Richard Branson went ahead to do the investment without the professor's report. You see, you can overanalyse until all opportunities pass you by. I have seen people, men and women, who overanalysed a prospect and could not make a headway with their lives. Now past 40, still single, they wished they analysed less. **Succeed before consciousness!**

Remember Damian Mark Smith's book "Do Nothing"? The sub title says, **STOP LOOKING, START LIVING.**

Chapter Fourteen

You are The Chief Meaning Officer of Your Life

Forces beyond your control can take away everything you possess except one thing, your freedom to choose how you will respond to the situation." **-Victor Frankl**

In an address at Silicon Valley to a gathering of 4300 would be founders and **CEO**s in 2015, the legendary **Jack Welch**, former **CEO** of General Electric told his audience that the job of the Chief Executive Officer is to make meaning. Jack Welch, in his speech titled the *"Real-Life MBA"* described the job of the **CEO** as *Chief Meaning Officer*. The clip of Jack Welch's speech can be found on YouTube.

You see, we are all Chief Meaning Officers for our individual lives. As **CEO**s of our destinies, we are the only ones that can make meanings out of everyday events in our lives. When we say our experience of life is from the inside out rather than from the outside in, we are exactly saying that we are the chief meaning officers of our lives. Many times, we do not know the awesome responsibility that this places on us. When we realize that life is a game of monopoly and we are the players actively doing the best that we can in any given moment, we will take increasing responsibility for the meanings that we create. We are not fully in control of this monopoly game called life, but one thing we can do is that whether we win or lose, we can decide to enjoy the game.

Victor Frankl was a holocaust survivor and medical doctor who founded the logotherapy and authored the book, *"Man's Search for Meaning"*. Frankl saw first-hand the gruesome murder of millions of people inside **NAZI** camps in Poland. In his book, Man's Search For Meaning, Frankl describes horrible agonies of sufferers in these death camps and how millions reached their death by finding no meaning in life; but he argues still that there were a handful of people who, in spite of the situation in the death camps, managed to find meaning in life. Below, I reproduce some of Frankl's quotes in his book, "Man's Search for Meaning".

"When we are no longer able to change a situation, we are challenged to change ourselves. Everything can be taken from a man but one thing: the last of the human freedoms—to choose one's attitude in any given set of circumstances, to choose one's own way."

"In some ways suffering ceases to be suffering at the moment it finds a meaning, such as the meaning of a sacrifice."

"Life is never made unbearable by circumstances, but only by lack of meaning and purpose."

"Forces beyond your control can take away everything you possess except one thing, your freedom to choose how you will respond to the situation."

   Viktor E. Frankl, Man's Search for Meaning

In 2017, I was at the Elevation Church in Lekki, Nigeria and I heard Pastor **Godman Akinlabi**, the lead pastor of the church say that *"the meanings we make about life are far more important than riches"*. Instantly, I knew what he meant. My daughter, Havilah was sitting by my side and I saw her write down the exact words on her notes. When we came out of the church, I asked her if she understood what the words meant? She tried her best to explain what she thought it meant, but I said to her that the day you find the real meaning of what Pastor Godman just said, your outlook on life will never be the same again.

You see, whether we are experiencing pain or happiness, we are the ones creating meaning from the everyday events that surround us. We can never abdicate our roles as chief meaning makers. As in monopoly, after the dice is cast, we do not know what card we will pick, but we can always decide to enjoy the game. Life is a game.

In his book, Seduced by Consciousness, Jack Pransky tells the story of a musician in the United States who married a very beautiful lady and shortly thereafter left for a musical performance that took him out of home for an extended period. One day he came back home and found his new wife with another man in his house. He was heartbroken. The wife begged for his forgiveness, promising that this will never happen again, and he forgave her. A month later, this musician caught the wife with another man and he was severely devastated. This musician lost all his confidence and became depressed. He wrote Jack Pransky seeking counsel. After identifying with his pain and struggles, Jack Pransky went on to explain in an email he sent to him that the way he sees this experience is what is more important for his mental wellbeing. Pransky explained that in any given situation several choices are available and each of these choices provide us with different states of mental wellbeing. He went on to suggest different ways that this musician might look at this situation.

- Thoughts of murder
- Total devastation: she ruined my life

- I can never trust another woman in my life
- This really sucks
- Well, that is the way life goes sometimes; luckily, I found out
- Compassion for her, as she grew up in a screwed-up family with few morals
- Hope, because a lot of good women are out there waiting to meet him
- I am going to be OK no matter what she did
- Gratefulness for the time he had with her when it was really good
- Total peace and love
- And many more possibilities.

Pransky, in his book went on to ask, which one is reality?

He concludes that there is no real way to think and that we make up whichever one we land on and then call it *"my life"*. We have that power to create whatever we call our life. We get the feeling or emotional experience of whichever one we create. No matter how "difficult" the situation we think we are in, in that same situation exist meaning making opportunities that can leave us worse off or in total joy.

Several years ago, I sat under Dr David Oyedepo giving a teaching on gratitude, I was in deep mental pain, but I heard the words, "give God praise, because, it could have been worse". Instantly, I saw a different possibility in my situation and I began to amend and gradually recovered.

Alibaba founder, **Jack Ma** is one of the richest people in the world, with a net worth of over $36 billion according to Forbes. But there was a time when he couldn't even get a job at Kentucky Fried Chicken. After college, Ma applied for 30 jobs in his home city of Hangzhou, China. He was rejected in all. At **KFC**, 24 people applied for the job, says Ma, and while 23 were hired — he wasn't. The same thing happened when he tried to be a cop. This time four of five applicants were hired, all except Ma. Another time Ma lost out on a job to his own blood. "My cousin and I waited for two hours in a long queue to be the waiter for the four-star hotel in my city, on a very hot day," he says. "My cousin's score was much lower than mine, but he was accepted, and I was rejected!"

Ma applied for an Australian visiting visa 7 times and was rejected. He applied to go to Harvard, 10 times and was rejected. Today, Ma gives speeches at Harvard and in one of his recent speeches in China, Australian Prime minister was one of Ma's audience.

You have to make meanings from your life events that propels you forward. Make meanings that give you energy and zest for life, not meanings that take the life out of you. Maybe you have thrown a monopoly dice and picked a card that says, **"GO TO JAIL"**, trust that this will not be the end and you will soon pick a card that says, ***"GET OUT OF JAIL AND COLLECT $200m"***.

"If you change the way you look at things, the things you look at will change." **– Dr Wayne Dyer**

Chapter Fifteen

Learning To Listen –
Strengthening Your Mental Resilience

*To access divine potential,
you will need a head (AI)
bypass surgery"*
– Dr Leroy Thompson

"Listen with curiosity. Speak with honesty. Act with integrity. The greatest problem with communication is we don't listen to understand. We listen to reply. When we listen with curiosity, we don't listen with the intent to reply. We listen for what's behind the words."

— **Roy T. Bennett,** the Light in the Heart

One of the advantages of learning how life works from the inside out rather than from outside in for me has been my increased ability to listen. Ability to listen to my wife, my kids, relatives, friends, colleagues, bosses and subordinates. Generally, because of a failure to recognize the Principle of separate realities, we do not really listen. I believe that over 50% of what is being said in a conversation is lost because people are not listening to one another. Yet, there is no greater predictor of your success and happiness in life better than your ability to listen. As you go up in your career, there is increased need for you to increase your ability to listen.

Amy Jen Su and **Muriel Maignan Wilkins** writing for **Harvard Business Review** says *"As your role grows in scale and influence, so too must your ability to listen. But listening is one of the toughest skills to master — and requires uncovering deeper barriers within oneself. The key, ironically, is to focus on yourself. While tactically there are many ways to strengthen your listening skills, you must focus on the deeper, internal issues at stake to really improve. Listening is a skill that enables you to align people, decisions, and agendas. You cannot have leadership presence without hearing what others have to say"*. Focus on your self during a conversation, focus on the thoughts going on in your head, focus on the meanings you are making.

What are some of the barriers within yourself during a conversation? Tuned to a different voice/reality? Sometimes we are involved in a conversation, but our mind is tuned to a different voice. A friend is excited about a new raise, he cannot just wait to share the experience with you, but your internal reality is just different. You are nothing near excitement, if anything you are internally weighed down with unpaid bills, a failed exam etc. As you begin to pay more attention to what reality you are living in and catch yourself not paying any attention to what is being said, practice taking your attention from that your reality and begin to tell yourself that you need to know the reality of this friend. What reality is he in? As you do, something awesome will begin to happen in you. You will be very present in the conversation and you get new insights from his/her reality that will improve your own experience in the moment.

As meaning makers with a big Library of **ARTIFICIAL INTELLIGENCE (AI)**, we have perception about almost every person we know, from spouse to kids, to friends, relatives and workplace relationship. How about the AI programming that says the boss is wicked? As soon as the boss dials your extension and tells you to come for a 5 minutes chat in his office; listen to all the voices running wild in your head – *"the selfish man has come again….idiot of a man….I know he doesn't like me after all, but I am going to pray him to Armageddon whether he likes it or not"* and on and on your internal voice keeps crying out. But you see that AI programming is not **REAL**. You will get to the meeting and be muttering *"finish and let me go"*. Here is what your **AI** doesn't tell you, you are the **ONLY** person with the unique meaning that you have stored in your **AI**.

Recently, I was listening to Dr. Dicken Berttinger give a lecture on how we experience life and he demonstrated that for every meaning we make there are over a million other possible meanings from the same event or interaction. As you begin to realize how life works in your daily encounters, as you walk to your boss office you will begin to tell your **AI** voice to be silent. Here is a thought experiment, the next time you hear your AI reeling out all these noises, just quietly speak to your AI voice, "shut up, the boss is just a human being like me and he has his internal struggles just like me and I am going to *LEARN* the reality from which he speaks". You will be amazed the kind of conversation you will have with the boss that day. You see, life is *spiritual* and as spirits we can really feel from a deeper part of us when someone is really listening. We develop stronger bonds with people who really listen to us; people who are present when we are talking to them.

As we studied under the principle of separate realities, we are all living in separate realities. That we are born of the same parent does not translate to having the same experience of our parents. When I didn't have this understanding, I used to wonder why everyone else didn't see what I was seeing about the organization. I will walk to a colleague and share my thoughts on a subject and he or she will just be staring at me, wondering if I have lost my mind. The reason we have made different meanings from everyday business of the organization is that our experience of the organization differs. Even within ourselves, our experience of the organization changes from day to day.

If you are like me, your **AI** has categorized every possible image. I see a person that looks like someone that I have known previously and instantly without any effort, I attribute all the AI of that known person to this one. Let's say the face, build and race or ethnicity matched someone I knew that my **AI** classified as troublesome. As soon as I get talking to the person, my AI begins to constantly warn me, *"remember that troublesome guy?*

This is how he looked; people like this are troublesome, remember that that they can pretend a lot, remember that they are deceivers.... Bla bla bla". You see, that kind of thinking won't foster any meaningful dialogue.

My wife once worked in a hospital in Northern Ireland with doctors from several countries. In that kind of multicultural setting, you hear doctors frame up expected behaviours based on countries of origin. A new doctor resumes and he is from India, instantly the doctors from Africa *"know"* the behaviours to expect, because their AI has written programs according to the experience they have of the last Indian doctor.

I told my wife while writing this book that she was fortunate to have a good **AI** programming of many of the doctors from other countries she worked with and that helped her see these other doctors from a better frame of mind and by implication better working relationship. I have come across people that my AI wrote off as not being of any good and those persons have gone on to make a huge success of their lives. They are living a far "better" life than me. I had to confess once when interviewing people that I needed to de-bias myself and separate myself from my **AI**, to listen with curiosity and not with the attitude that I know it already. Here I am conducting an interview, and the fellow walks in, and my **AI** says you know people like this are not smart. Where is my AI getting this information? From past programming of images and behaviours. Now, as soon as that voice comes up, I just speak to myself *"You do **NOT** know this person, listen to them to find out who they are"*.

Many people enter new relationships and never really enjoy the relationships because of internal dialogues inside the **AI** warning them of what similar images represent and the dangers they pose. Sometimes I meet a fellow whom I knew 10 years ago, and my **AI** classification labelled him as a cheat. As soon as the person begins a discussion about money or a business deal, my **AI** shouts loud: remember he is a thief and cheat, he is going to lie to you again. You see, your **AI** made these recordings to protect you against being harmed by this person ten years ago, is it possible this person is no longer that person that you knew ten years ago? This is also true for a person you knew 10 years ago and your AI makes record of the person as honest and decent; 10 years is a lot, you may fall into trouble if you think the AI classification is still valid.

I do not say to always ignore your AI but tell your AI that you want to really *listen* to this person. There are things that we all did 10 years ago, that we will never do again. In my faith parlance, we have repented and moved on. Is it possible that this person has repented and moved on or *unrepented*? We cannot know by listening to our past recordings. When we begin to practice de-biased listening, we get to the place where the *voice of our spirit* goes past our AI to tell us more about the person and to help us connect in ways far deeper than we can intellectually.

Everything you need in this world is in your spirit. All the money, resources, friends, connections you will ever need resides there; but to access it, you will have to do a *HEAD BYPASS SURGERY* – you will have to rely less on your AI programming. You see, our spirit knows *MUCH MORE* than our minds and is superior to the databank of **AI** that runs our lives. We have shut up this intuition with our overdependence on our **AI**. But as we practice better listening skills, we will hear the spirit voice that transcends our AI to tell us what to do in every area of our lives. That won't happen overnight, I must warn you; but as you practice de-biased listening, you will get better at it and eventually you will come to the place where you will begin to have effortless conversations that are deeply spiritual and refreshing.

Chapter Sixteen

Lean Not to Your Own Understanding

*The closer we are to heaven
the more conscious of hell
we become*
– Dr. Billy Graham

It is amazing how difficult it is to let go of your beliefs, concepts and knowledge. Growing up we amassed this reservoir of knowledge, which we have called *Artificial Intelligence (AI)* in the series of chapters in this book. When confronted with a challenge, we quickly call on this vast database of knowledge to help us out of the fix that we find ourselves. As the reader might rightly observe, there is nothing wrong with consulting this databank of knowledge. It seems just right to go back into memory and pull out what was our saving grace when we were in similar quagmire in times past.

The challenge for me is that this databank is very limited. It has a sensory library of coded experiences and knowledge that answers a very limited set of challenges. In a conference in London, I heard Dr Berttinger say that the total sum of what we know is less than one in a billion of the knowledge available in the world today. When I heard that *I sat properly*. Do you mean that with all my degrees and education all that I know is less than a billionth of what is possible? I tried to reason that what Dr Bettinger was saying is an exaggeration; but it really got me thinking. Even if what I know is one in a thousand of what is possible, my perspective on life shifted. Scientist say the most brilliant among us only uses 10% of the human brain. If I imagine that the likes of Steve Jobs got to 10%, it is possible that over five billion people use less than 1% of their brain. For me this speaks a lot. What is it to learn from this? It says to me that for every challenge that I face, my knowledge bank **(AI)** might only just have probability of 1 in a billion or thousands of coming up with the answer. This for me is humbling.

Dr Kenneth Copeland once said it is foolish to worry; saying that what you know will barely scratch the surface of the problem. He said, we should rather learn to rely more on God. I know this is not a religious write up, but *EVERYONE* on this planet believes in God in one way or the other. Your beliefs may not be exactly as mine, but at the end of the day, all humans believe in the existence of a higher power. Quantum physicist have been able to split the atom and even sub particles of the atom and they have reached the conclusion that all of life is powered by an intelligent life.

On July 2, 2018, the independent newspaper in London carried this stunning news headline, *"Scientists see planet being born for the first ever time"*. I was puzzled. You mean planets are giving birth to planets? I never knew this. The newspaper went on to say

"Scientists have seen a newborn star being formed for the first time ever. The stunning images, taken using the ESO's Very Large Telescope, offers an unprecedented view of the formation of planets. And the discovery could help us understand how planets are formed in much more detail than ever before. Until now, the act of planet formation has usually been hidden by a veil of dust. But in the new study astronomers led by a group at the Max

Planck Institute for Astronomy have finally been able to capture a spectacularly clear image of a planet breaking through the 'disc' from which it is formed. The pictures show the young planet, named PDS 70b, tearing its way through the planet-forming material that surrounds the young star.

We live in a universe of mysteries, but we are limited by the little knowledge we have. The point of this chapter is for us to prod ourselves to learn how to go past our understanding. The only reason we worry is that we cannot find an answer within our databank of knowledge. The only reason a person will commit suicide is that they reached the limit of what solutions are available in their knowledge bank. I once heard someone say that beyond a certain point, our knowledge becomes a disadvantage. I will guess that this is probably one of the reasons Paul was told in Acts 26:25 that his knowledge was making him mad. You see the more knowledge you have, the more difficult it is to let it go for something new. Doctors are required by their profession not to treat their relatives, because the knowledge of the possible outcomes that they possess calls their judgement into question as they have a dual interest in the treatment of their relatives.

Miracles seldom happen with highly intellectual people, because they think they know everything already. The story of Job in the bible is a very interesting one. Here was a man who was the epitome of knowledge. He could not understand why trouble befell him. From Job chapter 3 you read of the man spilling out *intellectual foolishness*. Hear the words of the man who represented the pinnacle of knowledge in his days in Job 3: 1- 13.

"After this, Job opened his mouth and cursed the day of his birth. 2 He said: 3

"May the day of my birth perish, and the night that said, 'A boy is conceived!' 4 That day—may it turn to darkness; may God above not care about it; may no light shine on it. 5 May gloom and utter darkness claim it once more; may a cloud settle over it; may blackness overwhelm it. 6 That night—may thick darkness seize it; may it not be included among the days of the year nor be entered in any of the months. 7 May that night be barren; may no shout of joy be heard in it. 8 May those who curse days curse that day, those who are ready to rouse Leviathan. 9 May its morning stars become dark; may it wait for daylight in vain and not see the first rays of dawn, 10 for it did not shut the doors of the womb on me to hide trouble from my eyes. 11 "Why did I not perish at birth, and die as I came from the womb? 12 Why were there knees to receive me and breasts that I might be nursed? 13 For now I would be lying down in peace; I would be asleep and at rest". His knowledge shut him in the ***prison of his thinking***.

Are you troubled today, distressed and depressed? Do not lean to your own understanding. Solomon was regarded as the wisest man that ever lived, hear what he has to say in Prov. 3: 5 -6 *"Trust in the Lord with all thine heart; and lean not unto thine own understanding. 6 In all thy ways acknowledge him, and he shall direct thy paths."* If you have done all that you know to do, you have done enough. Now go to sleep and let the powers that are beyond you go to work. If you worry, the powers will not go to work. You must cast your cares upon Him, because He cares for you.

As a 100L student at the University of Benin, I never ceased to be amazed by the manner with which Kekule came up with the formula for **Benzene**. For a long time, scientists could not come up with a formula for Benzene. The prevalent knowledge on valence theory and carbon bonding could not explain the behaviour of the compound. After working tirelessly on the formula, Kekule *slept off.* In his sleep, he found the formula for Benzene.

Read the web story of Kekule and his discovery of the benzene structure – "*In 1890, at the 25th anniversary of the benzene structure discovery, Friedrich August Kekulé, a German chemist, reminisced about his major accomplishments and told of two dreams that he had at key moments of his work. In his first dream, in 1865, he saw atoms dance around and link to one another. He awakened and immediately began to sketch what he saw in his dream. Later, Kekulé had another dream, in which he saw atoms dance around, then form themselves into strings, moving about in a snake-like fashion. This vision continued until the snake of atoms formed itself into an image of a snake eating its own tail. This dream gave Kekulé the idea of the cyclic structure of benzene1.*"

Could it be that you are labouring too much to get a solution to your challenge?

It might just be time to *go to sleep on the problem.* Art Williams built one of the largest insurance companies in the world, and here is his motto for living "*All you can do is all you can do and all you can do is ENOUGH*". Dr Kenneth Copeland was once on a long fast and his friend Dr Jerry Savelle came to him and said, "It is time to break that fast and go play tennis". Although shocked by the counsel, he chose not to lean on his understanding, but rather took it; stopped his long miracle fast and went to play tennis. Shortly after, the thing for which he was fasting forever came to him. I have read and heard of people who after years of worry and anxiety over child birth, suddenly conceived and gave birth when they stopped worrying. I have seen the same amongst job seekers and several other examples. When you have done all that you can do, it is worthwhile to cease from your own understanding.

Don't trust your feelings, as your feelings may just be wrong. **Dr Billy Graham** commenting on trusting your feelings says that the closer you are to heaven, the more conscious of hell you are. You are just a step away from your *"heaven"* even though your emotions and feelings are in the opposite direction. Joseph in the bible did not feel close to the throne the night before, but by the day he came out of prison, he ascended the throne. Companies and individuals have gone from being bankrupt to reaching the top of their industrial sectors. Go to sleep on that issue that has been of concern to you, cease from your labours and you will be *awoken by a Kekule dream in the morning*.

Chapter Seventeen

The Invisible Person Running Your Life

> *I do not understand what I do.*
> *For what I want to do I do not do, but*
> *what I hate I do. For I have the desire*
> *to do what is good, but I cannot*
> *carry it out."* – **Apostle Paul, Rm 7:15**

I want to introduce you to the person responsible for much of the decisions that you make, why you chose the wife or husband that you currently have, the job that you do, the friends that you have, the colours in your house, the car make that you prefer and so on. My reason for exploring this person in detail is that a person this powerful should be known, considering how much influence he wields on us. I know many of the decisions he is making are good for me, but there are some that he makes that I would want to influence. I do not like for example, letting him tell me when to eat or how far I can go in life. Here I am in my conscious mind, I want to lose weight, make more money, travel round the world; but after I decide that I will only eat so and so meal, this person tells me that I should forget that plan. I set goals to build a great company and he tells me those kinds of plans are not for people like me.

For much of the writings in this book I have referred to a mental program called artificial intelligence **AI**, which is working in the background and influencing our lives. This **AI** is very powerful and makes a lot of decisions for us that we are not even aware of. **Marianne Szegedy-Maszak**, writing for the **US News and World Report** has this to say, *"According to cognitive neuroscientists, we are conscious of only about 5 percent of our cognitive activity, so most of our decisions, actions, emotions, and behaviour depend on the 95 percent of brain activity that goes beyond our conscious awareness"*.

If you drive regularly, I am sure that you have had the experience of driving a few kilometres and unaware of when and how you did it. What was happening was that your **AI** just took control and gave the instructions on the lane to take, the speed to go at and what else you needed to do. How is the AI able to do this? When you were learning to drive, you wrote mental programs of why you drove the way you did, why you went at that speed and how you might react if you met something strange. Once your AI got the code, he didn't really need you again. Growing up for example, if you lived in a slum and raised by poor parents, every time you wanted a good toy, your father told you those beautiful toys are not for you; at first you resisted it, but after a while you accepted it and told your **AI** to make sure you never went near those fine toys again. Now your **AI** works round the clock to protect you from good toys.

There have been fears recently on the growth of artificial intelligence in the computer world. One of such persons who is afraid of the spread of AI is **Elon Musk**. Why is there fear and a call for legislation on the spread of **AI**s? **AI**s are not Robots. They are developed to *"think"*. A robot is programmed with a set of reactive instructions such as "if you hear this sound then do this...", if you come across an obstacle then do this and that. That makes robots dumb servants. This is not the case with **AI**. **AI**s are developed to think, to observe and come up with their solutions.

In 2017, when Google's "**DEEP MIND**", an AI developed by Google beat the world Chess champion, people started expressing worries on the future of **AI**. The amazing thing about **DEEP MIND** was that it learnt to play Chess just a few hours before playing with the world chess champion. An **AI** is loaded with a set of codes on how decisions are made, and it is then programmed to come up with its own decisions when faced with any challenge. When you say someone has 20 years' experience in playing Chess, an AI can play Chess repeatedly overnight and get a hundred years' experience in just 24 hours. One fear is this: will the computer industry preload for example an intelligence, to kill an enemy on an object and the object preloaded with **AI** becomes so experienced and goes after humans?

The above description of how **AI** works in the computer world is to drive home the point we are making about our own **AI** or what we call subconscious mind. At the beginning we told our subconscious mind what to do and how to watch over us, and it does it so well that we started relying on it. The challenge is that some of the instructions we gave it earlier in our lives are no longer relevant. When we told our subconscious that we were not meant for the good toys, it was our understanding at that time; we now want good toys. When we heard of marriage challenges and told our **AI** to keep us single, it was for a point in time. Now we want to get married and our AI is holding us back, breaking some of the useful connections that we are making to get married. Here we are in a training on how to do this and that and this supercomputer **AI** reminds us that it is not for us. I used to think that my subconscious was a robot I built that I could give instructions to, but now I am finding out that it is an **AI chipset** and it makes its own decisions irrespective of my conscious wants and desires.

We cannot do without our subconscious or AI. On several occasions, this AI has been our saving grace. We have walked into a place and even without thinking; our **AI** sounded a warning that something was wrong. Some of that warning wasn't specifically something that we taught our AI, but because the AI can utilize the basic rules we gave it to make decisions, even when we were not consciously aware of danger, our AI alerted us of the presence of danger. However, like the fears expressed by the likes of **Elon Musk** about computer **AIs**, how much control over our lives do we want to cede to our subconscious.

As in AI, can this subconscious get the better of us and harm us in any way? At a certain age you gave your AI a script for your alcohol consumption, because you enjoyed alcohol; and besides every time you drank it, your confidence was sky high; you sang on stage effortlessly. Now, your AI has developed several control codes by which you drink alcohol without even thinking and it is damaging your livers. You want to stop, but you do not just seem able to stop.

Growing up, a petty crime was the formula with which you got on. Your **AI** has now perfected how to do this for you and you can engage in petty crimes even without thinking about it. The positive side of our AI is that it is the reason we are hired to do the work we do. The vacancy says 20 years sales experience. If your AI has been taught well and has directed you well this past 20 years in selling, why do you want to ditch it?

In his book *"Blink, thinking without thinking"* **Malcom Gladwell** explains how we think without thinking. He narrates several stories of people who just by looking at something reached the exact conclusion within seconds. A conclusion an amateur reached only after months of examining the same object. Gladwell goes on to tell the story of policemen who shot a black victim because their AI was preloaded with prejudice, a decision which a policeman with a different programming will not reach. He explains that in times of pressure, we do not use our analytical conscious mind. A policeman who needs to make a decision in the fraction of a second whether to shoot at a suspect is not likely to have the time to analyse whether or not he should shoot. In a fraction of a second his AI takes control and makes the decision for him.

I remember asking the American Sport Psychologist, **Garret Kraemer** what he will do if he was confronted by a particular challenge? His answer shocked me. He said he wouldn't know what he will do because at the moment he confronts the challenge several options could come up and he wouldn't even be able to tell me which of them he would choose in the very moment. At first, I felt he avoided answering my question, but over time, since that experience, I have observed in my own life that I have made decisions in the spur of the moment which afterward I would not consider in my rational conscious mind. Today, I have humbled myself and I now pray even in matters I once was 100% sure what I will do. Where it is a conversation, I not only pray for myself but also for the person with whom I am going to have the conversation.

Chapter Eighteen

Self-Awareness

> *It's only when the conscious mind confronts the unconscious that a provisional reaction will ensue which determines the subsequent procedure."* – **Carl Jung**

In the last chapter, we started looking at this invisible personality that makes decision for us. Using current knowledge of Artificial intelligence, **AI**, to gain an understanding of this person, we saw how we can reach decisions that our conscious mind is not part of. The greater interest is how we might harness this understanding and I think this knowledge is best utilized in the understanding of ourselves – *gaining Self-awareness.*

Self-awareness is fast becoming a managerial essential in today's field of work. We are all more confident, make better decisions, have stronger relationships, communicate better and more creative when we are self-aware. The other day, I was in a meeting and a fellow told a story of how God had miraculously provided for him supernaturally. Immediately without even thinking, I said inside myself that these so-called testimonies are fake; but immediately I said this inside myself, I quickly caught me asking *the thinking*, where, how in the world did you reach that conclusion? I thought about the knowledge I have come to gain about the working of the subconscious and how the subconscious can reach decisions for you without your involvement.

As quickly as I had this realization, I decided to separate myself from the thinking that said the testimony was fake. I muttered to myself that the conclusion must have been reached in my deep past when I became rebellious about people telling stories about being helped by God and especially when I concluded that a lot of religious people were scams. That subconscious coding continued to reach decisions for me every time someone told a story of being healed or being miraculously provided for.

Immediately I distanced myself from my **AI**, I said in response, *"oh yes, that story is true"*. You needed to see the hair of my head stand, my brain circuitry running wild and wondering what had happened to me. What had actually just happened was that I was opposing my **AI**. I was taking charge of my personality. I cannot allow a program that I wrote become more powerful than me. I should be the one who takes the final responsibility for the decisions that I implement. In management, a CEO is not excused because the Excel program made a wrong profit calculation. That CEO must account for the error.

We too must learn to account for the final decisions that we make. I will tell you that the simple decision to oppose my AI in the moment of saying that a testimony wasn't a lie, was amazing to me. The knowledge was certainly worth a million dollars to me. I began to think of what had just happened and how I might utilize the knowledge of what had just happened to better understand how we might intervene on a need basis where our AI might be running our lives in a different direction from what we truly desire.

You see, we hardly read a story or reach an understanding with an open mind. Two people read a story on what the Government is doing, and both reach different conclusions on the same story. Why? There is a software underneath that is giving meaning to the input. If your software has been programmed to see everything being done by the government with suspicion, you will interpret even good intentions of the government with suspicion. The same applies to your place of work and even your relationships. Here and there, you are in a management meeting and that "untrustworthy" manager takes the stage; you instantly *"know"* he is going to lie because he is not trustworthy. You are a lady and here comes a man with great intentions to date and possibly make a serious marriage proposal to you, but as soon as he starts to speak, you instinctively hear him speak like that ex that spoke queen's English and it ended that everything he said was a lie, and because of the program running beneath the surface, you are unable to really commit to exploring him.

Even when you finally give in, you put yourself on edge watching out for signs that he is not different from that guy on which your AI script was written. Sometimes you go even so far as to marry this person, but the script keeps playing in the back ground; today you think you are in love and the next day you do not think so anymore. People want to be friends with you and without thinking you wave them off. There are people that you need to go meet yourself to build a friendship with, but your last attempt was viewed with suspicion and today, you do not ever go out of your way to build any friendship as you will be seen as too cheap.

Remember what we have been learning all along from lesson one? Any thought that says for example that going out of your way to introduce yourself to a person makes you cheap is internally self-created. Nobody can make you look cheap but **YOU**. You are the only one that can put that label on yourself. If your **AI** is running that subtle program today, you can un-write it, go make the friends you want to make, you will see your AI scream, but that is the beginning of Freedom from the dominance of a program that you unconsciously wrote.

To quote renowned psychologist **Carl Jung**, *"It's only when the conscious mind confronts the unconscious that a provisional reaction will ensue which determines the subsequent procedure."* You are going to confront every limiting belief that might be running in certain areas of your life. You are going to challenge them and write in their place what you now want to believe going forward. It is all in your power to do.

What is Self-consciousness? It is the training and ability to be able to monitor your inner world. To be able sit back and separate yourself from emotions and thought patterns that thrust themselves on you without your thinking; to be aware and present in the moment. When you increase in this training you will begin to distance yourself from some automatic emotions, fears and thought patterns that you do not want.

Here I am writing this chapter and a person I know just jumps into my thinking. The next thing, I begin to observe negative thinking about the person in my radar. I just stop and mutter inside me, *"those thoughts are not from me"*. I am Judgmental about something I know nothing about. Those thoughts are not from me. I am jealous of someone and even wishing them evil when I have no interaction with these persons to even warrant thinking about them. Surely, that is not me and I am **<u>NOT</u>** going to accept the thoughts. I get into a shopping mall and the guy working towards me looks like a cheat. How did I design what a cheat looks like? I know these are not my thoughts and that some program is trying to dump them on me; I try to look inward to when and how I created this code for my AI and I get this *aha* moment, it was a film I watched a while ago and the lead criminal walked exactly like this guy.

The trick to beginning to do what **Carl Jung** says is to become *<u>MORE PRESENT</u>* in your everyday life. Don't just live your life on the auto pilot of your subconscious; or allow your **AI** to be your default mode; even if your **AI** is right 99% of the time, just try to be more present when your **AI** is reaching its decisions. Don't be an absentee tenant in your own affairs. You are the landlord and you must exert your influence. In his book, *"The Inner Game of Selling"*, **Ron Willingham** has this to say, *"In our language, it's when our "I Think" confronts our "I Am," and challenges it to give us answers, that hunches, ideas, and insights begin to flow from the wisdom that permeates the deep recesses of our unconscious. This reaction can then automatically influence our outer behaviours"*. When we begin to watch interactions for which we were unconscious slaves, we will begin to get better insights into experiences that once frightened us.

Professor Timothy D Wilson of Virginia University is the author of the book *"Strangers to Ourselves"*. In it, he defines the unconscious as *"mental processes that are inaccessible to consciousness but that influence judgments, feelings, or behaviour."* Wilson went on to say concerning Self-awareness – *"People who are completely out of touch with their abilities, traits, and feelings are likely to be unhappy with themselves and* *insufferable around others. Indeed, a common definition of mental illness is a loss of touch with reality, including one's own traits and capabilities"*.

Some of the running codes buried in our subconscious include stories that we have innocently conjured from experiences of life. If you failed mathematics exam and you innocently stored the exam failure to mean that you will struggle with mathematics, your subconscious will work hard to make sure that you struggle with mathematics. The trick is to re-write that experience as a **one-off** event and not **formula** on how your tomorrow will emerge. We can never be 100% aware of what we do, but by increasingly being present to dialogue with our subconscious in areas that really matter to us, we will begin to unveil a great depth of riches hitherto unknown to us.

Chapter Nineteen

Springs of Action

> *I know, LORD, that a person's*
> *way of life is not his own;*
> *no one who walks*
> *determines his own steps"*
> **- Jeremiah 10:23**

In the last chapter, we began looking at how we can harness the understanding of the interaction of the conscious and the unconscious to better our lives or to our advantage. We peered into our automatic behaviours and explored ways that we might be able to dialogue with the complex networks of computational power going on in our sub conscious. Even when we are ourselves conscious, our **AI** does not stop working – it continues to supply the basis for the decisions that we make. It is like a corporate organization; even though the bulk stops at the desk of the **CEO**, he makes use of numbers crunched by the finance department, sales forecast supplied by marketing and production figures assembled by the manufacturing department to reach his judgement.

So, even though we claim that we are conscious at the level of understanding with which we are interacting, some other software is working underneath to give us basis for our conscious action. As I am writing right now, I am working on Microsoft Word, the plain sheet that I type on is just what I am conscious of; there are myriads of codes written to create Microsoft Word that I know nothing about to make it work. At the level of consciousness what I know about the workings of my laptop is less than 5% of what is really happening. The average smart phone user uses less than 10% of the phone capabilities and is at best only aware of 2% of how the phone works; yet at the conscious level he thinks he is in full control of the phone.

Many of us have witnessed scenarios where, in the course of using our laptops or smartphones, we suddenly see a pop up telling us that this device will have to reboot NOW, as there is an update that needs to be installed. How can this happen when we are the one consciously using the device? The reason is that the phone, like the subconscious, is interacting with a vast amount of hidden computational power and even a much bigger computing ecosystem called the Internet. Sometimes the vast power beyond the system gives us warning of a pending system reset, at some other times, no warning is given, a system reset is done without permission. In times of heavy risk, if you have a strong antivirus system which like our **AI** is always working to protect the device, it shuts down the device with such brutal force that you are just left wondering what is happening; then you see a red flag of a serious virus threat that you have escaped a malicious virus attack.

If by chance you are able to abort this forced shut down, you may end up having your system infected by a virus and depending on the type of virus that might just be the end of your system. It is amazing the similarities between the workings of our physical systems and that of our subconscious. Today, to help us recover data, we now save a lot our information on the cloud, a procedure that works the same way as our subconscious.

The difficulty in understanding this conscious – subconscious interaction is not something that started today. Every religion in one form or another encounters this challenge. In the Bible, the prophet Jeremiah had to exclaim *"LORD, I know that people's lives are not their own; it is not for them to direct their steps"*. He humbly admits that we are not fully responsible for the steps that we take. They say in psychology that 67% of our self-esteem, a key determinant of how far you will go in life is already set in our subconscious by the time we are 5. That is a lot for me to take in. By 5 years old I have decided nearly 70% of how far I want to go in life? I have programmed much of my future when I have not even started primary one? That is telling a lot for me and like Jeremiah, I wish to also exclaim *"LORD, I know that people's lives are not their own; it is not for them to direct their steps"*.

Somehow, I get frightened by how much I really control my life. My boasting and worries just look stupid when I concede that it is not in me to direct my path. As wise as Solomon was in the bible, he had to admit in Proverbs 20:24 "A man's steps are from the **LORD**, so how can anyone understand his own way?" The psychologist **EM Foster**, who was one of the pioneers of discovery writing – (a concept that says that authors do not just write because of what they plan to write, but in writing, the author begins to know what he thinks. That is until he started writing, the author did not really know what he thinks about the subject), had this to say *"How do I know what I think until I see what I say"*.

Today, Foster's quote has remained as one of the beacons of psychology. In my small life, I have written whole essays, when all I knew at the beginning was the topic, and as I wrote, I came to know what I believed. Even now, I very much doubt if I really knew the topic I thought I knew at the beginning. I believe that to the extent we are in control of our laptops, to the same extent we are in control of our lives.

The human ego loathes this understanding as it takes away our pride and all that we have constructed about our personality. It sounds very confusing when you have grown up in a free will school of thought – welcome to one of several mysteries about life – the more you know, the more you realize you do not know. Does this leave us orphans to a fate we have no role in? I do not personally think so, but the interaction is a very delicate one and many who are unable to fathom this delicate balance have almost made a shipwreck of their lives.

My personal construct on how to navigate this delicate balance will take me too deep into the realm of religion much beyond the scope of a secular writing of this kind; but suffice to say that we are not helpless in this interaction between the conscious and the subconscious. Solomon, after admitting that it was not in man to direct his path, went to say that "In all your ways, acknowledge him and he will bring your desires to pass" – Prov 3:6; Psalm 37:4. That for me gives one glimpse of the interaction between the conscious and the unconscious that **Carl Jung** spoke about. Our desires represent our conscious wants and needs. Solomon prescribes a formula by which conscious needs are met from our unconscious computing powers.

Several years ago, my friend was dating a girl and they were deeply in love and preparing for the wedding ceremony. From nowhere, the girl started complaining and after a week of complaining about this and that, she called off the wedding ceremonies. My friend was heartbroken and for a month he looked like someone that was mentally ill. Determined to get married, my friend awoke from slumber and six months later was in a new relationship. As wedding cards were coming off the press, this ex fiancée showed up in his house to apologize for terminating their relationship over six months ago. Is this a case of inability to know what one really wants? Another man screamed to his wife every day that the marriage was going to end. He woke up one morning and the wife has moved out. The man refused to eat all day saying that his wife was all that he had. Is it possible that many times we consciously are at variance with what is going on within our huge sub-consciousness?

Is there a psychological apparatus by which we might know upfront what we genuinely want? Psychologists say that we do not really know what we want. Is there a meter we might ask what our true wants are or exactly what programs we wrote before we were even conscious of writing these programs? *Like Computing codes that run our smartphones and laptops, many of these programs that run our lives cannot even be assessed from consciousness – the same way I cannot access the codes that make my MS Word run smoothly.* We fluctuate from day to day because of several complex interactions within us including moods, ego, AI etc. What do we really want and where do these wants spring from? James once asked in the bible James 4:1 *"What is causing the quarrels and fights among you? Don't they come from the evil desires at war within you?"* Solomon in Prov 4:23 *"Watch over your heart with all diligence, for from it flow the issues of life".*

Chapter Twenty

Creating Everyday Miracles - 1

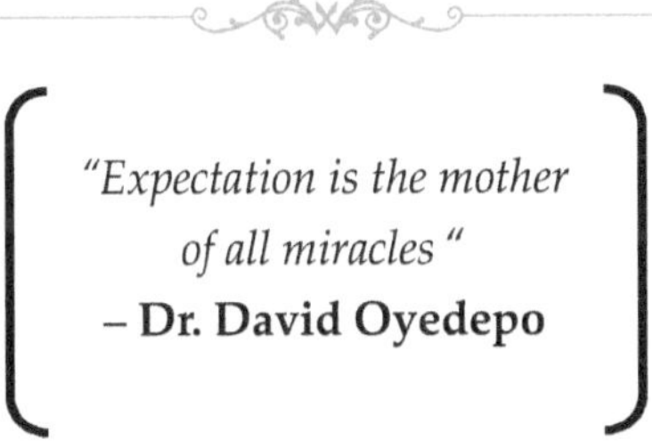

In the last chapter, we stretched the possibilities of our automatic behaviours and the springs from where they emanate. We are continuing this week to stretch the possibilities a little more. In the last two chapters, we examined ways to interact better with automatic behaviours that we did not consciously like even though admitting that some unconscious programming is not easily accessible to us. If we are the users of a laptop called *"our life"* which was given to us to experience and enjoy this world, it will be good to see how we can get this system working well. We stayed away from religious dimensions of the narrow interaction between the known and the unknown – we will continue to stay clear.

Drawing from that analogy, we know too well that we want our laptops performing well. Not everything that pops out from the web as we are browsing was authorized by us. What do we do in IT? We block the pop up and when our computer asks us whether it is a temporary blockage or a permanent blockage, we respond a yes or no. It is the same with our subconscious. I am checking my messages on Facebook and without my asking, Facebook brings me a post of a classmate of mine doing far greater and bigger things than me. A jealous voice rears its head in my thinking; and because we want our systems working smoothly we are determined to stamp out every virus attack. What did we say we will do in chapter 18? We learned to respond by saying "***that is not me***". That is just the result of a program I wrote possibly before I was 5 years old. Now my system is asking, "*Do you want to temporarily stop this pop up or you want to kill it permanently*? It is now up to me to decide. Simple? That is all I need to deal with unwanted thoughts. For some pop ups, I will say prevent site from creating new pages only now, while sometimes I just say "permanently". If we didn't have this knowledge, we may begin to feel condemned e.g. we are jealous, unforgiving etc.

What are the other types of pop up that we experience? The one that tells us we will be broke next week. Why do we experience this pop up? We have unconsciously believed that money will come to us through certain avenues and no more. Say we are salary earners, over time our subconscious knows how to help us spend what we receive. Over time we are bound by the constraints of that pay - check and we cannot see anything new. Once the pay-check is going down, our heart begins to pace in the grip of fear. What about the pop ups that come to us when we are going for interviews? We have attended 20 interviews already and it just seems like one after the other, there is just no hope. Soon we might even stop applying and accept that it is our fate to be jobless. But you see, your expectation sets your daily energy.

We have learnt in this series that life is internally self-created. If you have attended a thousand interviews, do not for once accept the pop up that tomorrow's own will just be the same. In 2004, I was a

Full-Time **MBA** student on self-sponsorship at the University College, Dublin – Republic of Ireland. Just four months into the program, surviving was becoming tough and I was on the lookout for just anything I could do to keep my family and myself afloat. I lived in a post-graduate hall housing six PG students per flat. I sent out approximately 10 job applications per day. As fast as I wrote the job applications, so too was the speed of the rejection letters. My flatmates became concerned if I was a *"fraudster-student"* living in their midst as 99% of all letters arriving in the flat were for me. It became normal for me to expect that every envelope contained *"we are sorry …."*

But you see, I refused to allow my AI to write the program that this will be the trajectory of my life. I woke up daily determined to get a new job. I went to project sites looking for some manual labour work to do. I was hungry. I had a wife and 4 kids to support, my fees were not fully paid, I was facing ejection threats for failure to pay my accommodation bills (**NB**: *I was finally ejected from Glenomena Hall, **UCD** in February 2004*), my wife was reading for her medical exams and looking after the kids; I just needed to do something. I received more rejections than I could possibly count, whether by post or physical interview. As I pressed, the day came, when the forces against me could no longer prevail, I got a night job as a protocol officer in the office of the University President. After my ejection from the luxurious **PG** hall, I moved into the undergraduate student hostel, which was much cheaper and continued my **MBA** studies.

Not long afterward, I got a consultancy assignment from a company that paid me amazing fees that made me forget I was a student. You see, you can refuse the temptation to just sit down and do nothing.

That you were rejected yesterday does not mean you will be rejected today. Always wake up with great expectations for everyday and you will begin to experience everyday miracles. Life is not a linear equation from your events of yesterday. If by any chance life has any linearity, it is this, *your tomorrow is directly proportional to the effort you put into life*. Understand what I am saying, life is not linearly proportional to your outcomes but to your heart attitude. In every failure, refine the fires of ambition and expand the dream.

Today, there are several stories about President Abraham Lincoln failing elections in every elective position until he contested for the United States Presidency and won. His success cannot be projected from the failures that occurred in his life but the effort that he put into life. Give life what it deserves today, don't just sit down thinking that there is nothing that you can do in the situation. There are a thousand and one things you can do. I know what it is like to have experienced a string of repeated failures in life - could be in relationships, finances etc. but what happened yesterday should not stop you from venturing today.

Nothing in the trajectory of Joseph in the bible projected him to be the prime minister of Egypt; but one day he woke up and **NEVER** returned to the prison. On a Facebook group that I belong to, a fellow asked Dr George Pransky, California based *"three principles"* practitioner if there was any way one can elevate his consciousness. I was glad to hear the response of Dr Pransky; he said, *"to elevate your consciousness, listen to voices that lift you up; voices that elevate you, voices that put a spring on your steps"*. In the days and weeks ahead, you will occasionally need these to help you reset your expectations; to wake every day and have a sense of purpose and not hopelessness.

I was listening to **Dr Chris Oyakhilome** one day and I heard him tell the story in the bible where Jesus told a man with no hands to stretch out his hands. Many of us will abuse and curse Jesus if we were the ones told to stretch out the very thing that we do not have. But you see, Dr Chris went on to say that as that man *"stretched his hand mentally"* his withered hand grew out. That just took me *"off my seat"*. The man mentally stretched out his hand and as he did it mentally, his physical hand was restored. You see, you can *mentally create your expectations*. Are you looking for a job, then do what people with jobs do. Wake up by 6am and go out of the house. If you have no means of transport just keep walking and telling the offices, organizations, people and shops that you come across what you can do. As you do that, it won't be long you will be doing the job that beats your imagination very soon.

In chapter 3, we dealt with the subject of shame. No one can make you experience shame but you. I don't know how many of us know the American athlete **Lance Armstrong**? His story is a comeback story of this decade. He was disgraced, de-robed and publicly humiliated just a few years ago. As I write, his comeback is making the headlines. Neurologists have found out that the brain is not a fixed entity incapable of changing. Your self-esteem set point may have been very low due to events that were beyond your choice when you were growing up and the environment in which you were raised; but that is not all the story about you; you can alter that set point. You can re-write your life story. That is why we said in chapter 19 that you should be very present when your AI is acting a script of your limitations, so you can either accept or reject them. When you understand what we are saying in these series of chapters, you will uncover a giant hidden inside you, buried in years of misunderstanding of how the human system works. That is what we are aiming to do in this series.

I know what it is like to be in one spot for so long. But, you can stretch out *that withered hand*. The man with the withered hand still believed his story can be turned around. A fellow sat by the pool of Bethesda for 38years. Psychologically speaking, this person cannot experience any change. The AI is so wired to keep him there for the rest of his life. But this man approached Jesus for a change of story. *I am not talking religion*; this man still believed that a change of story is possible. I bet that many of us have not experienced "*setbacks*" for even a year and yet we have thrown in the towel. If you have not been in one place for 38years and you are reading this article, then you can still experience a change of story. Just stretch out that withered hand and you will be made whole.

Chapter Twenty-one

Creating Everyday Miracles - 2

*The greatest discovery of my generation
is that a human being
can alter his life by altering
his attitudes."* **– William James**

If there is one thing we wish to accomplish in these chapters, it is to uncover the hidden potential that a misunderstanding of how life works has ignorantly deprived us of. We began part one of the topic – *"Creating Everyday Miracles"* in the last chapter. We saw that by altering our beliefs, we can tinker with our experience and maybe our life outcomes. We began to explore the possibility of altering deep-seated beliefs that have held us down over the ages. We ended the last chapter, by saying that we can even change the structure of our AI or brain programming.

Let me give you a small thought experience of how I altered a setting in my AI. I naturally drive fast a lot. I started driving at the age of 16 and as a young teen driving for the first time, I would just zap my dad's car and the neighbours will come complain to my dad how I almost rammed into their playing kids. I was always confident I could drive and never crash. That AI setting has run its course deep into my adult life. One day I was driving to work in the Republic of Ireland and a police officer stopped me for over speeding. I was given a fine to pay and points on my driving licence. Did you think that this altered my driving style? It sure did. I started learning to obey speed limits. You see, every old habit can be shattered. Every old limitation can be broken. My purpose of telling this story is to show you that we can change the computing powers that drive our lives. Being penalized for over speeding isn't a good way to change my AI but is sure shows that I can change my AI. What we wish to do is to have the brain reset without waiting for a police officer or accident or prison or divorce to bring about the changed behaviour.

As I have said previously, if we learn to be present and observe our automatic behaviours, we can question them and make some software upgrades. Growing up as a very shy and timid young boy, it just did not make sense that I could not approach young ladies. The day came when I decided to stretch out my withered hand. As a bachelor living in Lagos, I promised God to punish me if I ever fail to talk to a girl I liked because I was afraid or felt inadequate. Once that oath of action was sworn, I moved into action. It didn't bother me what I said, I just said anything, and that shyness left me. I dealt with my challenge in this area so much so, that when I met my wife, I did not beat about the bush; I went straight to the point. You too can demolish the hindrances keeping you on your bed all day. Get up and make stuff happen. Enough of an excuse-ridden life. You can get up and get going.

Legendary motivational speaker, **Jim Rohn** has this to say, "**Resolve** says, '*I will*.' The man says, '*I will climb this mountain. They told me it is too high, too far, too steep, too rocky and too difficult. But it's my mountain. I will climb it. You will soon see me waving from the top or dead on the side* *from trying.'"*. That is quite hard, but sometimes you need that force to alter a long overdue attachment to something that you do not wish to see again.

You can shatter the limiting belief that says you are too old to marry. That thought is not you, so don't act on it. At your current age, **DO YOU WANT TO MARRY**? Your conscious answer is what is important, not the program playing in you. You can terminate the limiting belief that makes you think your skin colour will not let you access some privileges. You can shatter the belief that you just might be too old for a new career. At 60 you can still do **ICAN** if that is your dream. *You see, all of life experiences are thought created*. If they are thought created, I want to create the ones that favour me. I want to wake up this morning expecting a million dollars in my bank account. *How will it happen? I don't know. Just the same way I don't know how I will end the day broke except that I am thinking it.* So, I choose to create an expectation that I desire.

Several years ago, Dr Kenneth E Hagin asked a sick fellow who came to him for prayers, "how long has this situation in your body been"? This was sometime in February of that year; and the lady replied by saying that by December it will be 2 years. Dr Hagin could not fathom how someone could project an unwanted situation into the future in this manner. You cannot be expecting to be free from an illness and have it in your mind that 10 months from now, you will be 2 years in the condition.

What we want to learn here is how to engage that programming that projects our lives to unwanted futures. When we are filled with news of *"no jobs"*, what do we do? That news is thought created. There is no such thing as "no jobs". When a bereaved/divorced woman continues with the AI program that tells her re-marriage is impossible, she becomes unkempt and obeys the AI that she is to remain single for the rest of her life; but this is just obedience to her AI and ignorance that she is acting up a script that she is possibly not aware of. The question isn't what your AI is saying? Do You Want to be married? You have as much chance of getting re-married as a man in that situation, but your AI is leading you wrongly. If **Meghan Markle** can re-marry and not just remarry, but someone her junior and a prince of the British Monarchy, what is holding you? The day you are liberated in thought, you will dress up for the next adventure of your life and it won't be long, you will be in the arms of your own Prince Harry. Do not say by December, I will be 3 years without so and so, stretch out the withered hand and open yourself to a life of miracles.

A lot of problems that we experience are thought created. Being overweight is a thought creation. You can take all the weight loss plans in the world – *(I have!)*; the day of your freedom will only come when you decide to disobey the *urges* that tell you to eat. They say it takes 21 days to change a habit; if you can disobey automatic urges to eat for this long and eat **ONLY** when you think in a conscious state that you really want to eat and for the right reasons that you have established, you are free from that weight. *You see a body of ocean waves, much of the sediments at the bottom are just at rest with all the swirling waves at the surface. The day you "dam" it, you will see the sediments at the bottom come to the surface.* All manner of things that you did not know to be there. **When you "dam" your automatic** *behaviours, a lot of unknown potentials begin to come alive. Once you "dam" the automatic urge to eat, your weight problem is history. The same goes for any habit that you wish to get rid of.*

Much of what people call mental health problems today are learned behaviours from obedience to a slavish **AI** master, who works to protect us with instructions we gave it without thinking of the consequences. I have experience of observing adolescent kids and seen how by paying attention to and heeding to hurtful and rebellious automatic voices they have nearly shipwrecked their lives. These are kids who are *perfectly well*, who in the rage of rebellion have exploited social media to take on strange masters for their souls. The day they realize how this whole life paradigm was created in the first place, they will forever be free and the instant of the moment, they will regain their total wellness.

A hurricane occurs when you try to dam moving ocean waves. When this occurs, you see a lot spilled into land from rising sea levels. *The resistance provided by the land dams the moving waves and you see energy of all kinds released.* There is huge potential in all of us, such potential that can remake us in entirely new ways that we have not even imagined, but the starting place is damming the automatic ocean waves that govern our lives. You are going to stand up to automatic behaviours that you do not want anymore. You wish to take a step and start a new venture and that voice rears in your head that you cannot do it. Like Jim Rohn said above, you are going to take action and stand up to that voice. I know a few successful people today whose beginning was nothing to write about.

Governor Ortom of Benue State started out as a motor park tout. Imagine for yourself what the average self-esteem of a motor park tout is, and you will go and study how these people changed the set point of their natural self-esteem. You must take action. Forget the feelings of emotions that would want to hinder you, these are normal, everyone who has made a success of his life has experienced these emotions. Do the new behaviour first and the new emotions will follow.

You can alter the trajectory of your thoughts and therefore your life. You can renew your mind. Only you can make the choice; no one can do it for you.

Chapter Twenty-two

Bouncing Back from Adversity

> *"It's your reaction to adversity,*
> *not adversity itself that*
> *determines how your life's story*
> *will develop."* **– Nelson Mandela**

I want to talk about implications of living a life from the inside out today. Of all the implications of living a life with the understanding that our moment-to-moment experience of life comes from the inside, there is none that I like as its capacity to make me more resilient. It might be something else for someone else, but for me, I have been really helped by this understanding. Knowledge of this understanding has helped me traverse some really difficult moments in my life. I will narrate my personal triumph using this understanding at some other time. Knowing that my moment-to-moment experience of life comes from my thinking in the moment has meant me bothering less about what people think about me, worries about status and acceptance.

Today I want to use a case study that is in public domain – Dismissed University of Ife Accounting Professor, **Richard Akindele**. I want to discuss options for resilience for one in the place of Professor Richard Akindele. Just to bring a few of us to date, Richard Akindele was dismissed by the University of Ife for demanding sex from

Monica Osagie as a reward for him to upgrade her exam scores. This is a Professor that is a married man and a Pastor with Children. I presume the professor should be about 60years of age. If my understanding is correct, when one is dismissed from his or her place of work, he is stripped of all terminal benefits.

By implication, much of the terminal cash flows of the professor, outside of his savings are just gone. I really sympathize with this professor; it is bad enough to lose your job this way, but the more traumatic part is having your kids, wife, family, church members and all the people that look up to you listen to that recorded conversation that went viral on social media. How do you face up to that humiliation? As a man, it is difficult to imagine a more traumatic event than that, except one has an understanding that keeps one above the turbulence.

In 2015 after data from the Canadian dating site *Ashley Madison* was hacked, a few of the names that came to the public knowledge committed suicide. One of such persons was Professor John Gibson. Gibson was a professor and Pastor at the New Orleans Baptist Church. Five days after Ashley Madison site was hacked, Gibson committed suicide, stating that he could not stand the humiliation.

Richard Akindele and John Gibson are so much alike. I have been thinking of Richard since he was dismissed from the University of Ife with a lot of empathy. Do I support what he did? Of course not. So why a lot of sympathy? This is because it is human to err. One of the strongest counsels from the Bible that readily comes to mind is *"Let him that think he stands take heed lest he fall"* This has increasingly impacted my mind-set in dealing with the failings of others over the years. My interest in life is to help people going through challenges and even now I really would love to get in touch with Professor Richard. How do you rebuild your life after an ordeal like this? First, I must congratulate him that he did not take the ignoble route of suicide; for me suicide is cowardice. One of the things that you will learn from living a life with an inside out understanding is that you will begin to show yourself more compassion. A lot of people can show others compassion but find it difficult to show themselves compassion.

Visit the link *http://money.cnn.com/2015/09/08/ technology/ashley-madison-suicide/index.html* and hear what Professor Gibson's family said about his suicide. His wife said for years, he preached a message that encouraged his church members to take hold of God's mercy and forgiveness, but he could not show himself the very mercy he preached. The daughter said she couldn't imagine why her father will think that she will not forgive him. He held himself to a standard that was unbiblical. In the same bible that he preached, Jesus said, *"let him that has not committed sin cast the first stone."*

Back to the case study of my dear brother, Richard Akindele. Here are my thoughts. He should honestly ask for forgiveness from his wife, children, church, and family members, everyone that looked up to him and from Monica Osagie. He might be lucky if his immediate family toe the line preached by the family of Gibson. I will suspect that they will forgive him if he has been a good father at home.

He must totally forgive Monica Osagie and decide to move on with his life. If he does not get forgiveness from his immediate family, which is a possibility; he can still move on. The key person in this entire saga is the professor himself. As we have come to know in this understanding, we are the one creating meanings from the events that happen. What meanings will he create? I will suggest he seeks out a place of solitude to calm all the muddled water. If he doubts his ability to manage the immediate impact – (I suspect by now he has passed this stage, which usually happens within the first two weeks) – he should take along with him to a solitary confinement a trusted friend who will show him nothing but **COMPASSION**. He should just relax and sleep for 1 week doing **NOTHING** until his mind is clear. If possible, take some good books with him, good books of *"come back"* stories. Find a book on Bill Clinton and Monica Lewinsky affair.

Thereafter he can create the following meaning. Tell the painful thoughts of guilt – I am the one manufacturing you. I tried to do something ignoble and it ended my academic career, but right now it is just my thoughts and I. My strength is not that I fell, but my ability to bounce back. I know hundred percent that this incident will work together for my good. I am too certain of that. The thoughts may not go at once, but they will eventually go. Just keep telling yourself that one year from now I will not even remember that this event ever happened. I am going to do greater things than I did before. I am going to challenge myself to make my life count. This might just be time to set up my own auditing firm or get a job in an auditing firm. This is the time for the professor to seek out biographies of people who came out of adversity and made their life count.

You see, the difficult challenge when something like this happens is your ability to put it in proper context. Every person living in the world today has done one bizarre thing at one point or another. It may not be a sex scandal, but whatever it is, we have all done things that we would never wish to be in the public domain. It is the reason Jesus said, "if you have not sinned cast the first stone". As I have written before, **SHAME** is a mental construct – It does not exist. Once you have your wild thoughts under control, I can assure you what you will do next will show up. Jesus told a woman **CAUGHT IN ADULTERY** – (Not different from Professor Richard Akindele, - Go and have a *NORMAL LIFE*.). You can always decide to have a normal life after a disaster.

A lot of people without this understanding take the path of cowardice. What will you do if you were Donald Trump, in a tightly fought election where you have been accused of sex abuse by several women and a new video comes out where you are boasting of your exploits? I remember watching Donald Trump the night after the leaked video, he was quite subdued. To be subdued is normal, it is the path of every normal person but like I have written previously, you get up and go do what you need to do *INSPITE* of. Donald Trump went for his next debate with Hillary Clinton. Even when opinion polls said the election was over, he ignored the inner voice that will come at a time like this to say, "Give up". He did not give up. Against all odds, Donald Trump emerged the President of the United States. Great **CEO**s and Generals know this. They know how to despise the inner voice that screams give up. There are several books and case studies of **CEO**s doing the impossible in unimaginable situations after devastating setbacks. You and I can learn from these. Bouncing back from adversity is a choice and we must choose to bounce back. We all can do it and we must do it. The next chapter of our life will tell of how we overcame.

Even in near defeats, great generals know that it is *NOT OVER UNTIL IT IS OVER*. Winston Churchill looked at a most difficult war and said, "**NEVER, NEVER GIVE UP**".

Chapter Twenty-three

Marriage & Relationships

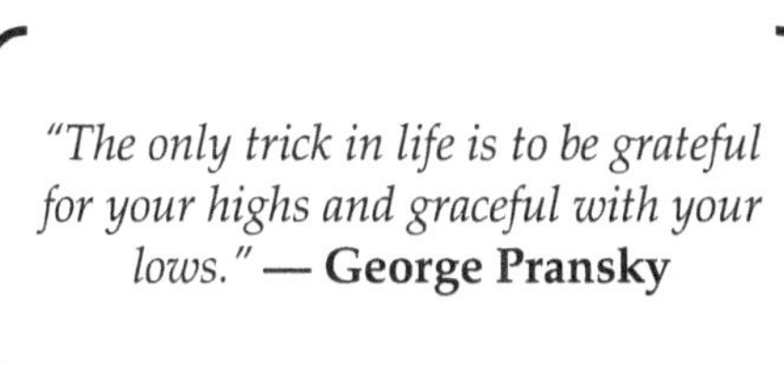

"The only trick in life is to be grateful for your highs and graceful with your lows." — **George Pransky**

Drawing from what we have learnt in the principle of separate realities, no two persons are in the same reality nor will ever be in the same reality all the time. The energy put in trying to change one another is therefore futile in a marriage relationship. A failure to recognise this simple fact has resulted in much heartbreak and marital stress.

Much of my understanding of marriage in the context of how life is experienced from the inside out rather than from the outside in is drawn from the book, "**The Relationship Handbook**" by **George Pransky**, PhD. In terms of utilizing the principles of learning to live from the inside - out, George Pransky's book is a great text on the subject; I strongly recommend it for couples or would be couples. On page 9 of the book, George had this to say, *"If you read this book with an open mind you will see there is an easy way to be together in a relationship. Maybe someday a child would ask "why were there so many unhappy marriages back in the 1990s and before?" Her parents might respond: "I don't really know. I guess people just didn't understand* *relationships in those days. I am so glad we have this understanding now"*. Pransky states further that the cause of marital problems is bad software, a misunderstanding of the deeper dynamics of a relationship.

(I am assuming that the reader has read the earlier chapters of this book and would have gotten a basic understanding of some of the terms we will be using in this article such as "software", "separate realities" etc.)

Pransky, a marriage counsellor for over forty years, in his book explores some common themes around which much misunderstanding lies. The first challenge is that of *incompatibility*. We are just incompatible – many couples will argue; but if you have been a reader of the previous chapters, with specific reference to the principle of *separate realities*, I will like you to reflect on the issue of incompatibility with that learning.

Viewed from our learning that we experience life based on our programmed way of looking at things and not the very things themselves, we can examine this issue a little further. Let's take the case of a couple where one likes to go to church and the other does not. Is this couple incompatible? One person will say yes, and a second person will say they complement one another. So, which one are they? Incompatible or complimentary? Our state of mental health will adjust based on the internal judgement we make in the moment. Incompatibility will evoke stress and discomfort while complementarity will evoke comradeship. Do we as free agents have a choice in the moment?

Before I continue the discourse on incompatibility, I will like to digress and talk a little bit about **MOODS**. Nothing affects the way we look at things in life like the mood that we are in. In an earlier article, I described our troubled thoughts like mud water in a glass. If you do nothing, the mood will settle, if you continually trouble the glass of mud water by interference, the mud water will remain for as long as you continue to interfere. One of the key masteries of life that many are not willing to subject themselves to is a self-awareness of their mood. I will strongly recommend the Harvard Business Review article, **LEAD FROM THE TOP OF THE MOOD ELEVATOR** by **Larry Senn**.

In the **HBR** article referenced above, Larry narrates the story of working into the office of a **CEO** of an energy company. This **CEO**, who is a fighter, was visibly downcast about some press publicity about the company. Larry knew for once that the **CEO**'s outlook was tainted by his mood and handed him a mood elevator card that shows how we might respond to the same situation under different moods.

You see, our moods are constantly changing from moment to moment and day to day. Many children often get worried when their parents show different reactions to the same behaviour. Parents who are not self-aware and who do not know how moods colour our outlook are blind to the fact that they are likely to respond differently to the same behaviour of their kids under different moods. The reality is that we see things from the moods that we are in. I have repeatedly argued in different forums that what self-awareness will do for you in a relationship, prayer alone (without hearing or heeding instructions from prayer) will not do it. Whether at work or at home, we must consistently practice the habit of seeing how our outlook on life is coloured by the moods that we are in. This is the reason many psychologists advise us not to make serious decisions in low moods.

In my small life in business, I have seen people I consider generals in business momentarily want to throw in the towel in low moods. These same people become lions just a day after when they are in good moods. You see, in high moods, we are full of energy, resourceful, inspired and curious. In low moods, we are judgemental, irritable, worried and victimized. In the Bible we read of the prophet Elijah; in his high mood, he boasted of what God could do and destroyed the prophets of Baal, but just a few days on, he was in a very low mood, on the run from Jezebel, he loathed his life and asked God to kill him saying that he was worse off than his fathers who did not come close to his experience with God.

We must learn how to manage ourselves. A lot of people do not know how to manage themselves. **Tony Schwartz** and **Catherine McCarthy's** article in the **Harvard Business Review "Manage your Energy, not your time"** is a good place to start from. If energy is defined in physics as the capacity to work, energy comes from four main wellsprings in human beings: the body, emotions, mind, and spirit, writes the authors. You cannot consistently float in low mood and expect to have a good relationship, whether work or marital.

Personally, I am convinced that the starting point for any successful relationship is **self-awareness** or self-regulation/control. If you don't know you, it is futile trying to know me. You can only love your neighbour as yourself.

Why does mood matter in our personal and business lives? Your thinking determines your moods, creates your own reality and drives your behaviours according to Larry Senn.

Back to our incompatibility question, George Pransky has this to say. *"Complimentary and incompatible are two conclusions about the same situation, two sides of the same coin. When differences are viewed with respect, partners are viewed as complimentary. The same differences viewed from a feeling of discontent, will make the partners seem incompatible. It is the feeling that makes the difference. Respect and affinity are the feelings that turn the personality differences into assets in a relationship. These feelings allow one person to learn from another. For example, let's say an outgoing woman is married to a quiet, reserved man. With an understanding of how we experience life from the inside out that couple will learn from each other rather than attempt to remake the other in his or her image. It is always humbling to realize that today's incompatibility was yesterday's "refreshing difference". The two perspectives are just one thought away."*

We all have mental images or software of what we want in a marriage. Unknown to us, when we are both talking of marital fulfilment we have different meanings – *thanks to separate realities of what fulfilment really means.* In high moods, the differences in expectations do not carry much weight; but in low moods these differences become **HUGE.**

There is no such thing as incompatibility in a marriage.

Incompatibility is a thought, a way we decide to process our thinking especially in low moods. It is noteworthy that what is labelled incompatible in one marriage is the source of strength in another marriage. Remember that our feelings follow our thinking. If we **THINK** of a particular trait to mean incompatibility, we immediately begin to feel the thoughts and all manner of behaviours can emanate from that thought, which if unchecked can lead to divorce.

Chapter Twenty-four

Helping Teenagers see Their Wholeness

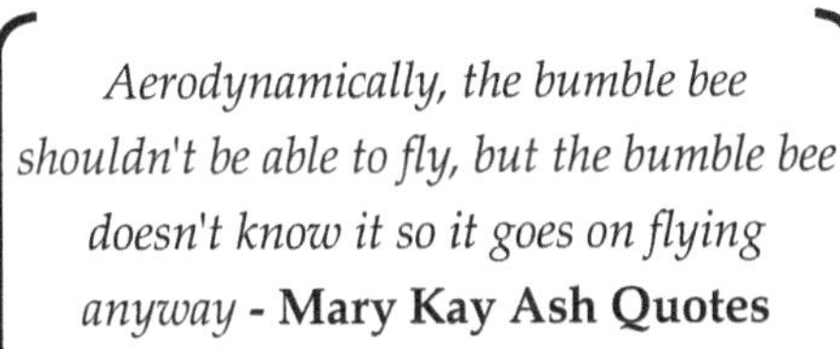

Aerodynamically, the bumble bee shouldn't be able to fly, but the bumble bee doesn't know it so it goes on flying anyway **- Mary Kay Ash Quotes**

I will begin this chapter by reproducing an article written by **Ralph Marston**, titled **Mental Momentum.**

"Which direction is your mental momentum headed? Are your thoughts joining together to support you or to hinder you?

Life has its ups and downs, its possibilities and problems. Which aspects are you focusing most of your mental energy around?

You're constantly creating elaborate scenarios about life that exist solely in your mind. Those scenarios, that mental momentum, can push your real-world life in a variety of directions.

If you seek to gather evidence that all of life is against you, you'll find it in abundance. Negative mental momentum will lend a destructive, neglectful, dejected flavour to all you do.

Choose instead to construct a scenario around the positive possibilities. Be thankful for the best that has been, imagine the best that can happen, and continue using the power of your thoughts to add details and substance.

Your actions, your effectiveness, your results are influenced by the mental state you're in. Maintain positive mental momentum and the benefits will flow to every part of your life"

The first question Ralph Marston asked is which aspect of your life are you focused on? We all have different zones in our lives. Some areas meet our desires while others do not. If every living person on the earth is faced with this dilemma, the next question that will naturally come to mind is why some persons appear to be in a state of continual joy while others appear to live in continual sadness. The answer is in what you focus on. So, if you are not happy today, the simple way to get out of that unhappiness is to change what you are focused on.

Some weeks ago, I was called upon to lead a prayer session in a church and the written prayer was handed to me by the pastor of the church. I had no time to read the short prayer before I took the microphone. As I started reading the prayer point, I got to the place where it said, "Oh God, we know these are hard times, please help our members to be able to go through these hard times". Something in me snapped; I just could not read it out, but the pastor had his eyes on me, so I stumbled and managed to mumble the words, but I did not believe the prayer. Are times really hard? It all depends on what you are focused on. Good times and bad times are both internal interpretations of the same scenario. "The good old days" as some will say is just an internal interpretation of reality.

Last week, I decided to listen to one of my favourite American speakers, the man Andrew Wommack, and I was really amazed at some of the things he spoke about. Andrew Wommack explained in his speech that 30 years ago, we just lived our lives and did the best we could, we were not aware that a crisis existed at midlife, but today, we hear things like "mid-life crisis" which our fathers knew nothing about. What are these teachings meant to do? The answer is simple, to teach us how to have a "mid-life" crisis. These so-called teachers of doom are ever formulating one thing or the other to impinge on people's consciousness. Today, we hear of "mental health crisis", a diagnosis that did not even exist 50 years ago. What is happening today? We are teaching people how to have a "mental health crisis". Once you teach people an illness and tell them how they will know they have it, and how the illness affects their life, they immediately become conscious of it and once you become conscious of anything you are hooked. Ask Apostle Paul in the Bible, "I did not know what was called sin until the law said, "thou shall not sin". In several of the past articles that we have examined on this series, we looked at the impact that consciousness has on our lives.

This is how the system works. I am a teenager just learning how to live my life. As a young boy, I decide to toast a girl for the first time and my efforts are rebuffed. I try again, and my efforts are rebuffed again. This is not funny, I always thought the world revolved around me and now I am getting a different message. This travail sends me into my secret cocoon and I momentarily begin to avoid young girls and begin to even doubt who I thought I was. My parents always told me I was the greatest "dude" in the world after God. Now that mystery is being challenged. In my temporary sadness, I come in contact with this social media post that list my sadness as one of the evidence that I am having mental illness. It sure looks appealing to me and helps to explain my situation. Once that consciousness is sown, I am hooked. An ignorant writer who is selling me sickness begins to convince me that I have other diseases of the mind that I am not aware. This seems subtle, but it is appealing to my current situation.

30 years ago, there was no social media, so a young boy who hits a brick wall momentarily feels the setback, goes into a cocoon but comes out stronger and launches a new attack on his target. Today, they go to Google to find out what is wrong with them and they meet a teacher of mental illness who sells them the idea that they are sick. Gradually, gradually, they begin to give heed to this seductive thought and accept another man's sickness as their sickness. Any thought that you think, you will begin to feel. I do not need anyone telling me about me. You cannot know me more than me. I am too complete to buy this junk. Unfortunately, many people are falling for this lie today and it is SAD. I am calling on my readers to help me wage a war against this evil called "mental health crisis". People need to be shown and taught how our experience of life is created. It is really urgent and I feel a burden to spread the message on our psychological wellbeing.

I end this chapter with another quote from Ralph Marston

"In this moment Do not wait to be beautiful. Be your beautiful... What you do today can improve all your tomorrows. Excellence is not a skill. It is an attitude. Beset by a difficult problem? Now is your chance to shine.
Pick yourself up, get to work and get triumphantly through it. If the world offers up negativity and despair, surprise the world by giving back love and kindness. Send out the energy that you wish to experience, and

you are certain to experience it. Happiness and fulfilment are alive in this moment. Allow them to flow freely and creatively through your life. Fall in love all over again with the miracle of being. Your imagination is great and magnificent, yet it cannot hold even a fraction of the possibilities".

"It's not the size of the dog in the fight; it's the size of the fight in the dog." — Mark Twain

Chapter Twenty-five

Release Your Strategic Reserves

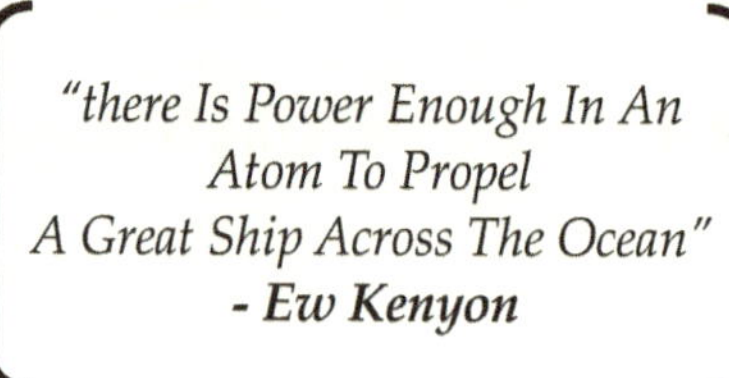

In the year 2018, I was in a particularly challenging negotiation in a transaction that could cost me much of everything I have worked for all my life. I was deeply troubled. I prayed, I reached for every kind of motivational material I could reach out for, but I remained restless. Somehow, I decided to just listen to an audio tape of the late inspirational speaker, **EW** Kenyon, titled **"IDENTIFICATION"**. I laid on the bed as if motionless. Intellectually, I knew that even if I lost everything I owned, it wasn't the end of my life, but experientially, I needed my mood changed, I wanted to be excited in spite of whatever outcome in this negotiation – the very core of most of my writings and teachings over the years. I barely heard what **EW** Kenyon was saying as my mind was loaded with all kinds of cares and anxieties. Suddenly I heard these words from the audio tape, **"THEY TELL US THAT THERE IS POWER ENOUGH IN AN ATOM TO PROPEL A GREAT SHIP ACROSS THE OCEAN"**. As I heard these words, I jumped off from the bed and my mood changed **INSTANTLY**.

I decided to pause the audio and be sure I heard exactly what I thought I heard. I put on my laptop and decided to search the **PDF** copy of the audio book, there it was on Page 22 under the chapter **"LIBERATING THE ABILITY OF GOD IN US"**. To be honest, you may not experience the same thing I experienced, but to this day those words have etched an indelible mark in my soul. As I got up from my self-pity and pity party sorrowful state, I was awakened to a new consciousness. You mean to say that there is enough power in a weightless thing like an atom to move an ocean liner across the sea? Look, I weigh over 100kg and I am imprisoned by the thoughts of a possible loss.

In a flicker, my prior thoughts now looked stupid. I put on my clothing and moved on with my life. I never called the company that was threatening me for the next six months – at this time they had much of my assets frozen and in their care. It never bothered me anymore if they seized everything I owned, what was important to me was how to put the myriads of atoms in my body to use. I realized I had much more resources that remained untapped than what I might possibly lose to this oppressive conglomerate with a myriad of very senior lawyers I am incapable of fighting by whatever means. In the natural, my resources and connections pale into insignificance when compared to this corporate behemoth.

Have you been reading the news recently? Have you been watching all the various news channels in recent weeks in the wake of Covid-19? Everything is looking gloomy. That is the work of the news media, so do not blame them. The news media does not get much traction with good news. The truth is that we are predisposed to imagine the worst outcome in every possibility that confronts us. I do not know why this is so, but this is just the way we have been wired. The buzz predictions are out there, and they are eating their innocent preys in the millions every day. Men's hearts are failing them, not because of what is going on but because of futuristic projections from the media that they are paying heed to. There is going to be massive job losses, hundreds of millions of persons will be laid off. Economies of nations will contract by 20% blab, blah, blah, and you hear it repeatedly and your heart shrinks. They tell you spend your money on only essentials and save for the rainy day because it is going to rain big time.

I will tell you the truth, these predictions are not $1 + 1 = 2$. These are not mathematical certainties. They are predictions based on our faulty brain wiring to always go for the worst-case scenario. Examine all the thoughts that frighten you, they are the worst-case scenarios in the given situation. In 2014, during the Ebola crisis the **CDC** projected that over a thousand deaths should be expected in the United States. President Obama immediately activated a response; 6,500 persons were trained by the **CDC** in readiness for this fight. How many deaths do you think occurred in the United States from Ebola? The answer is 4. My job here is not to criticize the **CDC**, they are doing a fantastic job. My job is to protect the mental health and wellbeing of the reader. Jesus admonishes us to be careful of the things we pay heed to. In the days of social media, men's hearts are going to fail because of what they are paying heed to. Whatever the knowledge or information you get on any subject, I wish to let you know that you still have a choice to decide whether you should pay heed to it – including this one that you are reading.

I have written a few articles where I have tried to use my layman's understanding of quantum physics to explain some everyday events and I would wish to draw your attention to a common thread in quantum physics – **IN ANY GIVEN CHALLENGE, THERE ARE INFINITE POSSIBILITIES; WHICH POSSIBILITY YOU EXPERIENCE IS DETERMINED BY YOUR AWARENESS**. In the current global pandemic, there are infinite possibilities that can become your experience and you have the power to decide the possibility that you wish to experience. I wish to influence you in this chapter to make a decision that liberates your abilities rather than imprison them. One of the greatest theorems in quantum physics is the "Heisenberg Uncertainty Principle" named after the famous German scientist, Werner Karl Heisenberg, 1901 -1976. Heisenberg's uncertainty principle was published in 1925 when Heisenberg was just 24 years of age; in 1932 Heisenberg, at 31 years of age won the Nobel Prize for physics. "The uncertainty principle says that we cannot measure the position (x) and the momentum (p) of a particle with absolute precision. The more accurately we know one of these values, the less accurately we know the other" – The Guardian Science, **UK**.

Here is the point I am bringing you to, the more accurate the **CDC** can predict what is happening with respect to Covid-19, the less we are able to predict what becomes of the economy tomorrow. This to the analytical mind is weird. The more you know about your situation, the less you can predict what will happen to you tomorrow.

To borrow from Jesus in "John 3:8, NIV:
"The wind blows wherever it pleases. You hear its sound, but you

cannot tell where it comes from or where it is going, so it is with everyone born of the Spirit"

You see, you are a spirit; that you hear the sound of a pandemic doesn't mean you can predict where it is going. You may have received your termination letter yesterday and you are afraid of how you might pay your mortgage; but here is the quantum reality – you can choose a new reality completely different from what the pandemic is telling you. Diagnosed of Cancer?

Ignore the predictions of your doctor; he does not know where you are going. Divorced and heartbroken?

Ignore the predictions of your psychologists and those of your friends – they have no clue that like Joseph you will wake up as the prime minister of Egypt tomorrow morning. Going by our mental calculations, it is impossible for one to be in prison today and wake up the day after as a prime minister. That is the life of the spirit, the uncertainty principle of Heisenberg at work. So, stop analysing and start living.

I do not wish to forget what brought me to this article, the revelation from **EW** Kenyon that a single atom in my body, if well understood can power an ocean liner across the Atlantic. If you really understood that a single idea that you can come up with during this pandemic can feed your entire city for 50 years, what will you pay heed to – the news of the pandemic or the appropriate working of your thoughts to your benefit and those of mankind?

The following excerpt has been taken from Grace International Church website on the connection between quantum science and spirituality **https://www.gci.org/articles/the-power-of-the-atom/**.

"If all the energy compacted in a small booklet could be released (it can't by any means known to science), it would supply enough energy to run a city about the size of San Diego, California, for 99 days. As you can see, the energy potential of matter is enormous! There was a dramatic demonstration of the power locked in the heart of the atom on Aug. 6, 1945. About 22 pounds (10 kilograms) of uranium were used in the atomic bomb that exploded over Hiroshima, Japan. Of that, it has been estimated that only a fraction of the mass of the uranium (about the size of a pea) was converted into energy. Humanity had learned how to unleash the awesome power of the atom."

There is tremendous untapped power locked in you and the world is waiting for it. Heisenberg played his part and many more have played their part up until this moment. This is an invitation for you to play your part. There is a quantum idea, if well harnessed from you right now, which can cause a doubling of the **GDP** of nations this year. Will you pay heed to it?

Chapter Twenty-six

You Can Choose Your Delusion or Placebo - Change Comes from the Inside

*Those who think they can
and those who think they can't are
both usually right."* **– Confucius**

Several years ago, I lived in Kano, Nigeria; my office was at 6A Ahmadu Bello Way, **GRA**, Kano, just 6 minutes' walk from the Governor's house. I enjoyed the serene environment. I don't know if the ambience is still the way it is then with the advent of gun wielding policemen and soldiers everywhere. I used to just walk past the Governors house on my way to work from Hotoro where I lived.

While I was in Kano, I had a very great friend, Mohammed who worked as a medical doctor in a nearby private hospital in Hotoro. As I will later find out, he was the junior partner in the clinic which he jointly owned with another doctor, Dr Ibrahim. The hospital was quite busy. Many of the indigenes of Hotoro loved the clinic, saying that the doctors were very brilliant. Fortunately, I never had need to go to the hospital for treatment while I lived in Kano, except social visits to see Dr Mohammed.

On a certain day, Mohammed visited me at home, and we had a very long conversation, I came to really know the guy I prided as my friend. Somehow as the conversation went on, I got to ask Mohammed the secret to their thriving clinic and he paused. Then he said something that shocked me. He said, "Tunde, I am not a doctor, I have a degree in Animal Science". I wasn't sure I heard him very well, and then he repeated what he just said again. He said "there is nothing to hide from you, what we do in the hospital is just give saline injections to everyone that comes to the clinic and tell them that they will begin to get well in under 1 hour and they go away believing what we tell them and they are well.

They prefer coming here and paying for the service than endless queues in the Government hospitals where they might not even be given the injections that they need". When I enquired if injections were better than the tablets that we took, he said "not really, but there are so many people in Kano who will not get well unless you give them injections and the people instinctively believe that injections work faster than tablets". When I sought to find out what was contained in the injections, Mohammed gave me another surprise, it was water mixed with salt.

For the first time in my life, I was faced with a phenomenon that I never heard of up until that time. How come saltwater injected into the body of sick patients cured a variety of ailments, with such effectiveness that attracted crowds to this hospital? For Mohammed did let me know that 85% of the patients usually got well within an hour. Could one's belief be that powerful to influence his health and possibly even the course of his life? Now read the story below taken from Dr Joe Dispenza's book, "You are the Placebo":

"In 1938, a 60-year-old man in rural Tennessee spent four months getting sicker and sicker, before his wife brought him to a 15-bed hospital at the edge of town. By this time, Vance Vanders (not his real name) had lost more than 50 pounds and appeared to be near death. The doctor, Drayton Doherty, suspected that Vanders was suffering from tuberculosis or possibly cancer, but repeated tests and x-rays came up negative. Dr. Doherty's physical examination showed nothing that could be causing Vanders's distress. Vanders refused to eat, so he was given a feeding tube, but he stubbornly vomited whatever was put down the tube.

He continued to get worse, repeating the conviction that he was going to die, and eventually he was barely able to talk. The end seemed near, although Dr. Doherty still had no idea what the man's affliction was. Vanders's distraught wife asked to speak to Dr. Doherty privately and, swearing him to secrecy, told him that her husband's problem was that he'd been "voodoo'd." It seems that Vanders, who lived in a community where voodoo was a common practice, had an argument with a local voodoo priest. The priest had summoned Vanders to the cemetery late one night, where he put a hex on the man by waving a bottle of malodorous liquid in front of Vanders's face. The priest told Vanders that he would soon die and that no one could save him.

That was it. Vanders was convinced that his days were numbered and thus believed in a new, dismal future reality. The defeated man returned home and refused to eat. Eventually, his wife brought him to the hospital. After Dr. Doherty had heard the whole story, he came up with a rather unorthodox plan for treating his patient.

In the morning, he summoned Vanders's family to his bedside and told them that he was now certain that he knew how to cure the sick man. The family listened intently as Dr. Doherty spun the following fabricated tale. He said that on the previous night, he had gone to the cemetery, where he'd tricked the voodoo priest into meeting with him and divulging how he had voodoo'd Vanders. It hadn't been easy, Dr. Doherty said.

The priest had understandably not wanted to cooperate, although he finally relented once Dr. Doherty had pinned him against a tree and choked him. Dr. Doherty said that the priest had told him that he'd rubbed some lizard eggs onto Vanders's skin and that the eggs had found their way to Vanders's stomach, where they'd hatched. Most of the lizards had died, but a large one had survived and was now eating Vanders's body from the inside out.

The doctor announced that all he had to do was remove the lizard from Vanders's body and the man would be cured. He then called for the nurse, who dutifully brought a large syringe filled with what Dr. Doherty claimed was a powerful medicine. In truth, the syringe was filled with a drug that induced vomiting.

Dr. Doherty carefully inspected the syringe to make sure it was working right and then ceremoniously injected his frightened patient with the fluid. In a grand gesture, he left the room, not saying another word to the stunned family. It wasn't long before the patient began to vomit. The nurse provided a basin and Vanders heaved, wailed, and retched for a time.

At a point that Dr. Doherty judged to be near the end of the vomiting, he confidently strode back into the room. Nearing the bedside, he reached into his black doctor's bag and scooped up a green lizard, hiding it in his palm beyond anyone's notice. Then just as Vanders vomited again, Dr. Doherty slipped the reptile into the basin. "Look, Vance!" he immediately cried out with all the drama he could muster. "Look what has come out of you. You are now cured. The voodoo curse is lifted!"

The room was buzzing. Some family members fell to the floor, moaning. Vanders himself jumped back away from the basin, in a wide-eyed daze. Within a few minutes, he'd fallen into a deep sleep that lasted more than 12 hours. When Vanders finally awoke, he was very hungry and eagerly consumed so much food that the doctor feared his stomach would burst. Within a week, the patient had regained all his weight and strength. He left the hospital a well man and lived at least another ten years.

Is it possible that a man could just curl up and die simply because he thought he'd been hexed? Does the contemporary witch doctor, adorned with a stethoscope and holding a prescription pad, speak with the same conviction for us as the voodoo priest did for Vanders—and is our belief the same? And if it's indeed true that a person could, on one level, just decide to die, then could it also be true that a person with a terminal disease could make the decision to live?

Can someone permanently change his or her internal state—dropping his or her identity as a cancer or arthritis victim or a heart patient or a person with Parkinson's—and simply walk into a healthy body just as easily as shedding one set of clothes and donning another?"

My conclusion is this: Every person living in this planet lives in their self-created beliefs. For some their beliefs are empowering and makes them happy, while for others, their beliefs are disempowering and works against them. Both are self-created beliefs. Don't you think it's time you created beliefs that empower and work for you? At the end of the day, it costs nothing, and it takes the same energy

Chapter Twenty-seven

Fasting & Humility –
The Magical Language of Every Religion - 1

Let's discuss fasting! This is one of the weapons of **LIFE** that I did not understand early enough in my life. What is fasting? It is abstinence from food for spiritual reasons. It is not dieting. Dieting can sometimes be at cross purposes with fasting. In dieting, when you abstain from food, you are trying to exert will power to bring down your weight. This is very good and brings some amount of discipline to your life; but this is not the same as fasting for spiritual purposes. In fasting, you are not celebrating what your will power can accomplish; you are giving up all of your will power and basking in your utter helplessness.

Why do you need to take yourself to a place of helplessness when all we learn from self-help books, motivational speakers and much of life is how to exert our will to do great things and become the next big thing in town? You fast because you wish to acknowledge that there is a creator behind this beautiful life that we see today. This Creator, God, hates pride and boasting, but unfortunately, as humans, pride and boasting is an integral part of us. We are naturally competitive. All our schools teach us this sport, to come **FIRST** is what our parents taught us in primary school. We got rewarded by daddy for coming first and trumping the other "lazy kids". We drive our beautiful limousine past a rickety car and we naturally feel great. We are born into opulence and we just naturally feel superior to the person born in poverty. But if we were to be sober, we would ask ourselves what exactly did we do to be born into wealth? Nothing!

We come into this world with certain perceived advantages - beauty, wealth, intelligence, power, special gifts etc. None of these things were achieved by our own power or ability. We just received them. These same natural endowments are some of the things that make us high headed. One woman gets married and immediately she is pregnant and gives birth to 1, 2, 3 and 4 sons. Another gets married and has challenges giving birth. In our way of thinking, the one with 4 sons is going to feel superior to the other woman. What is the unique contribution from any of these women having these kids? Nothing! We are naturally boastful of how wealthy we are, how brilliant we are etc., yet God declares absolutely in His word, **I HATE PRIDE**, Prov 8:13. The Bible goes on to say in 1Cor 4:7, "For who makes you different from anyone else? What do you have that you did not receive? And if you did receive it, why do you boast as though you did not receive it?"

Knowing that it is natural for us to be proud, what is the solution? The solution is to humble ourselves with fasting.

Can anyone live this life without pride or arrogance? I personally do not think so. If there is blood flowing through your veins, you will suffer from pride in one way or the other even if momentarily. You will come first in class and declare victory over others and proclaim that you have attained this by your might. You will be voted the most beautiful girl in your school and the day after, nobody can approach you again. If we are naturally this way, what is the way out? The way out is to continuously humble yourself – turning the prized possession to the one who gave it to us. You can successfully humble yourself with or without fasting, but from time to time, the glories of our prized possessions we are endued with will make us haughty. Even after we become humble, the humility will bestow certain blessings on you and when these blessings begin to come, you will not be able to hold the pride that will accompany the success. It is a vicious circle – perhaps that is why energy comes in a sinusoidal wave form, energy travels in peaks and valleys.

Pride of the heart cannot be eliminated so long as you are in this body; but you can manage it. Trying to eliminate it is trying to kill yourself. Even in a good thing that you do, your heart can become very proud. You may build the biggest company in the world and that achievement can become your greatest undoing if you do not manage the pride of success that accompanies that achievement. You may run a hospital with no bills, pay the school fees of orphans and so on and the very act of that good deed, becomes a source of pride in your life.

Irrespective of which religion you belong to, I have found out that every religion practice fasting. Even people who are not in any religion occasionally proclaim a fast to appeal to a "superior" power. Steve Jobs fasted often, Mohandas Karamchand Gandhi, popularly known as Mahatma Gandhi or The Father of the Nation of India, undertook 17 fasts during India's freedom movement. His longest fasts lasted 21 days. Fasting was a weapon used by Gandhi as part of his philosophy of Ahimsa (non-violence) as well as satyagraha. Ghandi used fasting to appeal to a higher power to intervene in India. You too should use it.

To be truly successful and **STAY** successful, you must therefore undertake deliberate fast to channel your energy wave form. It is one certain way to tame the beast of pride in our flesh and keep the flow of God's goodness in our lives continually. In fasting, we take a deliberate posture to renounce all our so-called self-accomplishments. We decide with our mouth and action to tell God that we are not the one that achieved these things but Him.

I do not know why but fasting and humility answers to everyone (in a measured sense) who undertakes it irrespective of their religion. I have therefore come to conclude that fasting is like gravity, it works magic to anyone who will employ it. We cannot avoid it if we want to see the unceasing goodness of **LIFE**. Are you going through any tough time today? **FAST** and Humble yourself. It doesn't matter what you may have done, if you will humble yourself with fasting, things can be turned around very quickly. King Ahab is reckoned to be the most wicked king in the bible and God decided to move against him for his wickedness. How did Ahab respond to God's sentence? He fasted and humbled himself before God.

1Kings 21: 17 – 28

17 Then the word of the Lord came to Elijah the Tishbite:
18 "Go down to meet Ahab king of Israel, who rules in Samaria. He is now in

Naboth's vineyard, where he has gone to take possession of it.

19 Say to him, 'This is what the Lord says: Have you not murdered a man and seized his property?' Then say to him, 'This is what the Lord says: In the place where dogs licked up Naboth's blood, dogs will lick up your blood—yes, yours!'"

20 Ahab said to Elijah, "So you have found me, my enemy!"

"I have found you," he answered, "because you have sold yourself to do evil in the eyes of the Lord.

21 He says, 'I am going to bring disaster on you. I will wipe out your descendants and cut off from Ahab every last male in Israel—slave or free.[a]

22 I will make your house like that of Jeroboam son of Nebat and that of Baasha son of Ahijah, because you have aroused my anger and have caused Israel to sin.'

23 "And also concerning Jezebel the Lord says: 'Dogs will devour Jezebel by the wall of[b] Jezreel.'

24 "Dogs will eat those belonging to Ahab who die in the city, and the birds will feed on those who die in the country."

25 (There was never anyone like Ahab, who sold himself to do evil in the eyes of the Lord, urged on by Jezebel his wife. 26 He behaved in the vilest manner by going after idols, like the Amorites the Lord drove out before Israel.)

27 When Ahab heard these words, he tore his clothes, put on sackcloth and fasted. He lay in sackcloth and went around meekly.

28 Then the word of the Lord came to Elijah the Tishbite: 29 "Have you noticed how Ahab has humbled himself before me? Because he has humbled himself, I will not bring this disaster in his day, but I will bring it on his house in the days of his son."

It does not matter the life you may have lived before now; my guess is that you are not likely to have done anything worse than Ahab did. It was God who testified of Ahab's wickedness. "There was never anyone like Ahab, who sold himself to do evil in the eyes of the Lord, urged on by Jezebel his wife". Ahab repented with fasting and God averted the planned disaster that was meant for Ahab. See how God makes a U turn when we repent of our arrogance. God said of Ahab's fasting ""Have you noticed how Ahab has **HUMBLED** himself before me?" You & I can also turn around any situation for which you desire a change.

Chapter Twenty-eight

Fasting & Humility –
The Magical Language of Every Religion - 2

*"Oh Lord it's hard to be humble
When you're perfect in
every way"* **-Mac Davis**

God was the one who made Ahab King, but the vicious circle kicks in. God gives us a gift and before long, the gift makes us think ourselves to be superior to others and God gets angry.

Jesus specifically teaches 'Blessed are the meek, for they shall inherit the kingdom of God'. The end objective of fasting is to bring about meekness, humility before **GOD**. If your fasting does not bring about any humility it may just be hunger strike. Fasting leads to self-abasement, humility, meekness. Many times, like the destruction meted on Ahab, we are afflicted when we have become arrogant. Read what the Psalmist says in Psalm 119: 67,71 "Before I was afflicted, I went astray, but now I obey your word. It was good for me to be afflicted so that I might learn your decrees".

Don't let your good works make you lose sight of the need for continual humility. Like I said before, our good deeds will bring increase of every kind and when that increase comes, we will become haughty again. This was the problem that Job had in the bible. He did a lot of good things and was rewarded as a result. But when he became wealthy, he reasoned that his good deeds have brought him this greatness. He could not see that God was responsible for his increase anymore.

In his affliction, he continued to hold on to his guns insisting that he has done no wrong, proclaiming all his good works. You must take every step, both in words and in deeds to make sure that your good works have not gotten to your head. If God does not give you the money, will you boast about how many people you have given scholarships to? If God does not give you good health, will you be alive to make those proclamations that you are making?

The heart of man is very deceptive. But during a fast, we can unearth all the deceits. We can open layers of pretense, hypocrisy and self-righteousness. Job did so much good that even God said of Job that he was blameless and feared God. After God blessed Job because of his good works, Job became proud and haughty and calamity came upon him. For many of us going through difficulties in our personal life, this is the most difficult sin to unravel. The ability to see that our curse is the result of our "self-righteousness".

When Job was afflicted, 3 friends came to console him. Job was the religious example of everything that anyone might desire. He was upright, helped the poor, defended the powerless and his good deeds were known to all. Those three friends could not really diagnose how Job might get out of his predicament. Repeatedly, Job declared his innocence, proclaiming in Job 27:6 *"My righteousness I hold fast, and will not let it go: my heart shall not reproach me so long as I live."*

Job continued to swear that he has never slept with another woman, he has never taken what belongs to another man, he has been eyes to the blind… and on and on. His three friends could not help. I would wish that Job knew that our self-righteousness was like filthy rags Isaiah 64:6. Can you imagine that someone in bad need of redemption is holding fast to dirty rags that caused his sickness in the first place?

Elihu was a young man who knew about the secret sins of the heart and the folly of anyone holding fast to his righteousness. Elihu comes to correct Job and his friends. He tells Job to keep his righteousness to himself. He rebukes Job for relying on his good works and holding on to filthy rags. He draws Job's attention to the fact that no one is free from the hidden sins of the heart and that the path to freedom was for man to lay hold on God's righteousness.

In Psalm 19 12-14, the psalmist *writes*
*"Who can discern his errors? Forgive my hidden faults. Keep your servant also from willful sins; may they not rule over me. Then will I be blameless, innocent of great transgression. May the words of my mouth and the meditation of my heart be pleasing in your sight, **O LORD**, my Rock and my Redeemer."*

Job should have known the limitations of human willpower. Elihu gives Job a proper perspective of life, Job 33: 8-12. Finally, God shows up and sharply rebukes Job and his three friends for not knowing what the problem is. From a self-proclaimed righteous man, Job acknowledges his pride and falls before God in repentance, Job 42:6 "Wherefore I abhor myself, and repent in dust and ashes". From a very high estimation of his credentials, Job suddenly hated his self-righteousness and God healed him and restored twice as much of all that Job lost. James says in the New Testament, that God showed mercy to Job. James 5:11

Fasting coupled with humility is a spiritual cure that will restore anyone to wholeness. Like I said before, it does not matter what you have done in time past, fasting and humility will restore you swiftly.

The book of Esther shows how Modercai's fast caused the King to remember a good deed he did that was long forgotten; how Esther, Mordecai and the rest of the Jews fasted and overthrew the wicked plans of Haman. It shows us too that we can use fasting to undo any wickedness that is directed at us. I am convinced that we will never understand all the spiritual laws that cause things to happen the way they do, however fasting and humility coupled with prayers can always turn things in our favor.

In Genesis 29, Leah apparently marries Jacob by deception, but if you follow the way events reveal themselves in the scriptures, this is likely because Rachel had become full of pride. Imagine being Leah, you are the senior sister and your younger one is deeply loved and preparing for marriage. In the ordinary lives of women, Rachel had all the reason to become proud. God sees this and moves Laban to give Leah to Jacob instead of Rachel. This is not all, God shuts Rachel's womb for her pride until the pride is destroyed. In the entire Bible, whenever a wife was hated, and her mate is loved and she becomes proud, the womb of the one that is loved is shut by God until there is humility. Genesis 29:31 "When the **LORD** saw that Leah was not loved, he enabled her to conceive, but Rachel

remained childless."
In 1Samuel, Hannah is loved while her mate is hated, and God shut the womb of Hannah and open the womb of her mate. In verse 6, her mate begins to mock her, and Hannah became miserable and decided to fast and humble herself; and the Lord opened her womb and Hannah gave birth to Samuel. I see a cyclical behavior that can only be managed by intentional fasting and humility. If this intentional fasting and humility is not there, we are bound to stay in our pain longer than necessary.

For this reason, I have equally concluded that no lineage can hold on to any advantage in perpetuity. Your humility today will bring you to wealth and the wealth will bring arrogance and that arrogance will be meted with judgement. You can however avert the judgement by regular fasting and prayer. Judge yourself instead of waiting for the judgement of God to bring you to justice. 1Cor11:31 "If we judge ourselves, we will not be judged". Fasting is akin to judging oneself.

Chapter Twenty-nine

Fasting & Humility –
The Magical Language of Every Religion - 3

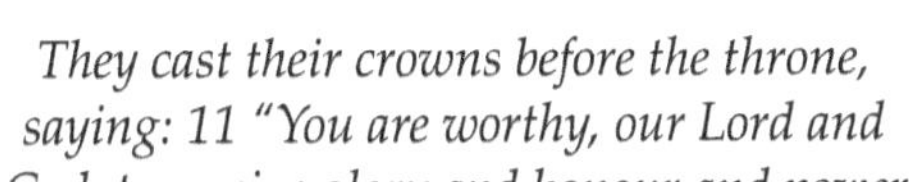

> *They cast their crowns before the throne, saying: 11 "You are worthy, our Lord and God, to receive glory and honour and power, for you created all things; by Your will they exist, and came to be."* **Rev 4: 10-11**

Fasting is a means to judge yourself and avoid being judged. A great literary icon and one of my mentors once said, "It is not God's responsibility to humble you, He already commanded you to humble yourself, but if you will not, he will humiliate you". Nebuchadnezzar is one such person that refused to humble himself despite several warnings. In the end, God decided to humiliate him.

Daniel 4: 20 -37

"The tree you saw, which grew and became strong, so that its top reached to heaven, and it was visible to the end of the whole earth, 21 whose leaves were beautiful and its fruit abundant, and in which was food for all, under which beasts of the field found shade, and in whose branches the birds of the heavens lived— 22 it is you, O king, who have grown and become strong. Your greatness has grown and reaches to heaven, and your dominion to the ends of the earth. 23 And because the king saw a watcher, a holy one, coming down from heaven and saying, 'Chop down the tree and destroy it, but leave the stump of its roots in the earth, bound with a band of iron and bronze, in the tender grass of the field, and let him be wet with the dew of heaven, and let his

portion be with the beasts of the field, till seven periods of time pass over him,' 24 this is the interpretation, O king: It is a decree of the Most High, which has come upon my lord the king, 25 that you shall be driven from among men, and your dwelling shall be with the beasts of the field. You shall be made to eat grass like an ox, and you shall be wet with the dew of heaven, and seven periods of time shall pass over you, till you know that the Most High rules the kingdom of men and gives it to whom he will. 26 And as it was commanded to leave the stump of the roots of the tree, your kingdom shall be confirmed for you from the time that you know that Heaven rules. 27 Therefore, O king, let my counsel be acceptable to you: break off your sins by practicing righteousness, and your iniquities by showing mercy to the oppressed, that there may perhaps be a lengthening of your prosperity." 28 All this came upon King Nebuchadnezzar. 29 At the end of twelve months he was walking on the roof of the royal palace of Babylon, 30 and the king answered and said, "Is not this great Babylon, which I have built by my mighty power as a royal residence and for the glory of my majesty?" 31 While the words were still in the king's mouth, there fell a voice from heaven, "O King Nebuchadnezzar, to you it is spoken: The kingdom has departed from you, 32 and you shall be driven from among men, and your dwelling shall be with the beasts of the field. And you shall be made to eat grass like an ox, and seven periods of time shall pass over you, until you know that the Most High rules the kingdom of men and gives it to whom he will." 33 Immediately the word was fulfilled against Nebuchadnezzar. He was driven from among men and ate grass like an ox, and his body was wet with the dew of heaven till his hair grew as long as eagles' feathers, and his nails were like birds' claws. 34 At the end of the days I, Nebuchadnezzar, lifted my eyes to heaven, and my reason returned to me, and I blessed the Most High, and praised and honored him who lives forever, for his dominion is an everlasting dominion, and his kingdom endures from generation to generation; 35 all the inhabitants of the earth are accounted as nothing, and he does according to his will among the host of heaven and among the inhabitants of the earth; and none can stay his hand or say to him, "What have you done?" 36 At the same time my reason returned to me, and for the glory of my kingdom, my majesty and splendor returned to me. My counselors and my lords sought me, and I was established in my kingdom, and still more greatness was added to me. 37 Now I, Nebuchadnezzar, praise and extol and honor the King of heaven, for all his works are right and his ways are just; and those who walk in pride he is able to humble."

King Nebuchadnezzar's conclusion after he was restored is startling "And those who walk in **PRIDE HE IS ABLE TO HUMBLE**". If Nebuchadnezzar was restored by fasting and humility, so will you and I. Jonah was one prophet who never really understood why God made a U turn when people fasted and humbled themselves. He would refuse to prophesy to Nineveh because he thought more about his integrity than God's right to be God.

He said, look God, I know you, you will say you will punish people and the same you will bless them when they repent. Finally, Jonah went to Nineveh and declares God's punishment for their evil ways. Immediately, the people of Nineveh proclaimed a fast to avert God's impending judgement. Jonah 3: 5 -10:

"5 The Ninevites believed God. A fast was proclaimed, and all of them, from the greatest to the least, put on sackcloth. 6 When Jonah's warning reached the king of Nineveh, he rose from his throne, took off his royal robes, covered himself with sackcloth and sat down in the dust. 7 This is the proclamation he issued in Nineveh: "By the decree of the king and his nobles: Do not let

people or animals, herds or flocks, taste anything; do not let them eat or drink. 8 But let people and animals be covered with sackcloth. Let everyone call urgently on God. Let them give up their evil ways and their violence. 9 Who knows? God may yet relent and with compassion turn from his fierce anger so that we will not perish." 10 When God saw what they did and how they turned from their evil ways, he relented and did not bring on them the destruction he had threatened".

Can you imagine the kind of repentance in Nineveh? Even their young ones and cattle fasted. My friend, fasting and prayer is the shortest route to avoid calamity. Jonah was really angry, but he did not know anything about God's righteousness. Jonah 4:

"4 But to Jonah this seemed very wrong, and he became angry. 2 He prayed to the Lord, "Isn't this what I said, Lord, when I was still at home? That is what I tried to forestall by fleeing to Tarshish. I knew that you are a gracious and compassionate God, slow to anger and abounding in love, a God who relents from sending calamity. 3 Now, Lord, take away my life, for it is better for me to die than to live." 4 But the Lord replied, "Is it right for you to be angry?" 5 Jonah had gone out and sat down at a place east of the city. There he made himself a shelter, sat in its shade and waited to see what would happen to the city. 6 Then the Lord God provided a leafy plant[a] and made it grow up over Jonah to give shade for his head to ease his discomfort, and Jonah was very happy about the plant. 7 But at dawn the next day God provided a worm, which chewed the plant so that it withered. 8 When the sun rose, God provided a scorching east wind, and the sun blazed on Jonah's head so that he grew faint. He wanted to die, and said, "It would be better for me to die than to live." 9 But God said to Jonah, "Is it right for you to be angry about the plant?" "It is," he said. "And I'm so angry I wish I were dead." 10 But the Lord said, "You have been concerned about this plant, though you did not tend it or make it grow. It sprang up overnight and died overnight. 11 And should I not have concern for the great city of Nineveh, in which there are more than a hundred and twenty thousand people who cannot tell their right hand from their left—and many animals?"

Chapter Thirty

Breaking The Habit of Being Yourself – Associative Memories

> *"We First Make Our Habits and*
> *Then Our Habits Make Us".*
> ***Tryon Edwards.***
> *Habit is a cable. —We weave a thread*
> *of it every day, and at last we*
> *cannot break it. —H. Mann.*

Stretch your thinking, possibly drawing from your own life and imagine how a man sitting at one spot for 38 years and not getting the healing he wants will be thinking. From my personal life, the probability that he can imagine himself to be healed someday is one in a billion. What is the impact of this way of thinking? This is the agony of the story of the man by the pool of Bethesda in the bible – John 5: 1-16.

The man may be the only one awake in the night when an angel comes to stir the water, but he will **NOT** throw himself into the pool because his brain is now wired to believe that he can **NEVER** be the first one to jump into the water. He will see the angel, watch the stirring of the water, then disapprove of himself. Sooner or later, he will tell himself that it was not even an angel after all; maybe a big fish stirred the water.

Remember the story of the "soured grapes"? The **HUNGRY** fox tries unsuccessfully to eat grapes from a vine, after repeated failures, the fox writes a neurological code of comfort that the grapes were sour anyway. How do you conclude that grapes that you did not even eat are sour? How many of us today are like this?

The man by the pool of Bethesda is not different from a man or woman who experiences marriage in a certain way and writes a code of comfort that he/she takes as reality; or a child growing up in a home who writes a code of comfort that gives him/her escape from the home experience. A person tries unsuccessfully to be married, then writes a code, "marriages are worse than hell anyway". And once the belief is actioned repeatedly, it becomes a habit, once a habit is formed you have relinquished your power to the habit, as we say in this book, your **AI.**

You wrote a mathematics examination in primary school, unprepared because there was no light at home, you failed. It so happened that this failure was wrongly coded in your brain, because just the same time you wrote the examination, you lost someone dear to you. Now as a child, these two events are unrelated; but by the law of associative memories, when you remember one of these events, the other kicks in.

Every time the maths teacher comes, you remember the loss of your close relative and it appears both are linked. Somehow you are now struggling with mathematics in school; but as a child you are unable to unearth the functioning of your neural wiring. You end up just encoding your brain with hatred for mathematics. Many reading this article can remember how that certain music takes them to a place and point in their lives. Yet the music has nothing to do with that experience.

Kenny Rogers sang his beautiful country music far away in the United States, but there are still songs in his albums that take me to a place and time in Edo State, Nigeria. You remember where you were on February 14, 2000 because on this valentine day, your boyfriend gave you a ring – you were at the Radisson Blue hotel in Victoria Island. To this day the Radisson Blue Hotel is to you the best hotel in the universe. Your belief about the Radisson Blue hotel does not really have anything to do with the hotel, it is just the law of associative meaning at work.

Getting a ring from your first boyfriend was a lifetime dream, the emotions that followed the event to this day still linger; and this took place at the Radisson Blue hotel. You can never forget this. For this reason, you have come to think well about the Radisson blue hotel. The reverse emotions will equally linger if you broke up at the Radisson blue hotel. You will hate the hotel for reasons which the hotel has no role. Every time you hear Radisson Hotel, you will remember all the trauma that you had to endure on the very day your relationship ended on a very sad note.

I am past 53 years, but I only just found out that the strange feelings I have in my mouth when a person with foul odour is around me is not due to their odour. For years, I wondered why my wife will not feel what I felt and she struggled to get what I was talking about. We will be in a restaurant and suddenly this strange odour smelling fellow walks in; we both perceive the bad odour and are in a hurry to get out of the restaurant. Once out, my wife forgets the bad odour, but for me, my mouth continues to salivate or secrete an uncomfortable chemical.

In January 2020, I was studying how the mind signals the brain and discovered that this experience was my mind signalling my brain to activate a familiar saved response to an unpleasant smell. Before now, I will go get a drink, say Coke or Pepsi, drink it so that it will replace the unpleasant chemical secretion in my mouth. Many times, I will even go and eat something with plenty of spices to kill the chemical secretion and with all of this, this unpleasant feeling will continue in my mouth for over an hour.

In recent times, after learning how we call up unconscious programming and how neurological wirings can activate chemicals in our body – (read Dr. Joe Dispensa's book – you are the Placebo), I finally understood what is happening. In just 3 weeks after I stopped taking any drink or eating food that I did not need in my body to suppress a chemical release in my mouth when I smell foul odours, it is amazing how this knowledge is changing my response to foul odours.

Previously, it could take me up to an hour to get past the chemical secretions in my mouth and that was with a lot of drinking or eating intermittently during the interval. I still feel the chemical secretions right now when a person with a foul odour is around me, but in a reduced intensity, but knowing what happens in my associative memory and signalling, I don't take any drink or eat any food anymore and within minutes, the feeling is gone.

For several years, the designer perfume "Fahrenheit Dior" was number 1 on my list of quality perfumes. All that changed some 20 years ago when during the burial of an uncle of mine, my cousin brought loads of Fahrenheit Dior and for over six hours was spraying the corpse of his late father. At the beginning, I was excited that my favourite perfume saturated the atmosphere; but this was a death that rocked a lot of what I believed about life at that time.

I went from excitement to irritation. As the casket was being lowered and my cousin emptied more and more bottles of the perfume on the corpse, I was nauseated and for nearly 10 years, I never could use Fahrenheit Dior again, because anytime I smelt the perfume, I unconsciously called up memories of my agony during the burial.

What are the associative memories that you have built up? Memories long buried and forgotten that have now come to shape your life. We are all living in a mind made delusion, some we really do not like, but we feel incapable of getting past them because we have no recollection of how they came about. If we conduct a deep search, we might be able to unearth them. You fear public speaking because your first trial when you were in secondary school left you publicly shamed. Your brain coded that shame in a small chemical compound and closed the possibility of ever doing public speaking again.

Is it possible that you can unearth that closed loop and write a new code? I invited a friend to a political gathering recently; he told me he was there because of my persuasion and that he will not for any reason accept any political appointment in Nigeria. Is it possible that he has reached this conclusion because of a wrong associative memory? Is it possible that when he remembers becoming a

Minister, sad associative memories of a minister he once knew begin to evolve?

I am not saying everyone will want to be a minister, I am only trying to unlock potentials that we might have buried because a wrong interpretation of life circumstances. Could it be that your hatred for tall men is just a wrongly coded associative memory? I have seen people who grew up rebelling against constituted authority and when I try to help them unearth the underlying reason, there is an associative memory that associates authority with attempts to control them. I know that you have repeatedly convinced yourself that all that you need is a roof over your head and no more.

Is it possible that this neural coding has been wrongly done? Have you thought of the millions of helpless people that you could help if you took off this limitation and allowed yourself to be another Bill Gates? Could the coding to refuse wealth or a ministerial appointment be the case of the "sour grapes"?

A habit does not form in one instant of action. Like a foot path, you need to walk this path a few times repeatedly. Many of us have read the stories of an elephant chained to a pole who after trying unsuccessfully for a few weeks to move outside the radius of the chain finally resolves not to try; even after the chain is removed, it decides not to try again.

What is happening to the elephant at the neurological level? As the elephant tries to go past the confines of the chain that is holding it, memories of the restrictions and the pain of the chain around him begin to evolve and he quickly relapses to safe known habitual patterns of behaviour. Once this new neurological way of thinking kicks in, a habit has been formed. Once the habit is formed, the elephant has "lost" control of his life to his habits. The greatest progress you can ever make in your life will only come IF you can break the habits that currently define you.

Chapter Thirty-one

Breaking The Habit of Being Yourself – 3

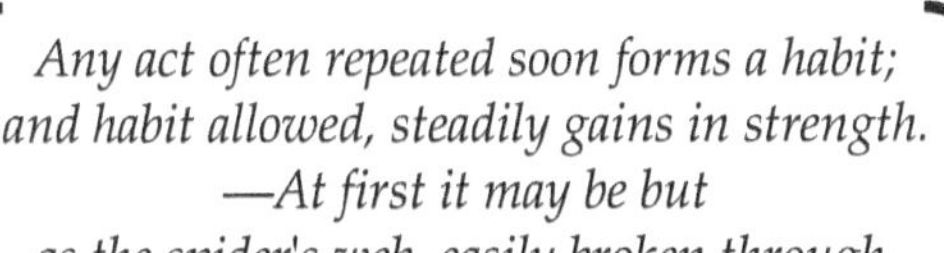

*Any act often repeated soon forms a habit;
and habit allowed, steadily gains in strength.
—At first it may be but
as the spider's web, easily broken through,
but if not resisted it soon binds
us with chains of steel"* —**Tryon Edwards.**

In several performance reviews of large and structured organizations, it is not uncommon to hear interviewing managers telling the person they are interviewing that he or she is good in "**A,B,C,D,E**" but they miss it in "**F**". The interviewing manager goes on to say, "look, your sectional head will be transferred to California next year, the position will then become open, but management has noticed that you shy away from confronting issues and are not likely to vote for your candidacy to fill the vacancy unless you change this signature character. I will be having another review with you in six months' time just to see how much you have changed along this line and update you with the thinking of management".

Six months down the line, the managerial perception has not changed. The candidate knows that nothing has really changed and that all the efforts have not yielded much. I know of a lady who would often confess her temperamental failure and go home crying that she is unable to do anything about it. These are two scenarios in a long list of habits that we are all accustomed to that are sabotaging our growth plans.

For a casual observer who has never intentionally confronted a habit, this should be a simple thing to deal with; but if he/she is honest enough to introspect some habits that needs changing, he/she will be quick to confess that this is not something that is easily accomplished at the intellectual level. To change that habit or any habit for that matter, you must become another person.

Quantum physics is finally making complex biblical miracles understandable to the human mind. Making a habit change is not different from receiving a biblical miracle. To accept to work **BY FAITH**, you must take on a new personality different from your analytical mind. The two work the same way.

To experience a miracle, you must come out of the analytical personality that you have built up over the years. By the time a person is 35 years of age, much of his/her life is a set of repeated behaviours. Go to bed on the same side of the bed that you are used to, wake up the same time, do the same routine, keep touch with the same friends, avoid unknowns that make you uncomfortable and so on. But this kind of life will not give you the kind of quantum change that you need to make a change of habit. You will need to come out of this life and embrace a new life. To quote Albert Einstein, "we cannot solve our problems with the same thinking that created them". We have to embrace a new reality. We have to become a new person.

Why will it be difficult for a person who desperately wants a promotion to make a much-needed change? The reason is not farfetched. At the neurological level, the person has become wired to a set of behaviours for a given stimuli. This wiring has built a certain zone of comfort and anytime the person wants to do something else, the neurons begin to scream. The screaming is so intense that unless one is sufficiently schooled in what is taking place, he/she runs back to the comfort zone and retreats.

Some of us have read stories of young girls who committed suicide after being raped; but we all know that not all raped girls commit suicide. So, what has happened at the neurological level? The way the neurons of the girl has her personality wired has been altered by the rape. We all have a personality wired inside us and breaking the habit of who we are involves breaking the neurological wiring unconsciously running our lives.

I once had a great friend who was on drugs. When he got "born again", he decided to quit. Previously, he started his day by 6am with a wrap of heroin, another by 12 and two more before going to bed. The day after his "born again" experience, he stayed away from drugs all day successfully, this continued for a few more days; but by the fifth day, he took two wraps instead of 4. He kept working on eliminating this habit, but as he explained to me, this looks utterly impossible. I did not know what I know now at that time, I might have helped him better. I counselled and prayed but he continued with his drug intake at a reduced consumption.

After attending a Sunday service one morning, he said he was done with drugs. For two whole days, he did not take any drugs, by the third day he was screaming my name, shouting that if he did not take his "wraps", he was going to go insane. What was happening to him can be explained with Dr Joe Dispenza's definition of a habit – *"an act you have practiced so much that your body knows how to do it better than your mind"* – at this point you have lost your mind to your body. Although your mind has proclaimed liberty, it is not aware that the body is the new master.

I worked in a certain company some years ago. The company has been in existence for more than 40 years and many of the staff at the time have spent varying amount of time at the company ranging from 5 to 30 years. Suddenly the company began to experience financial problems and had to lay off 70% of its workforce. Despite the company's poor culture, many of the staff who was laid off continued to hold prayer sessions for the company to re-absorb them.

They weren't praying for the company's resurgence because of their love for it, they were praying for the company's resurgence because the company was for them, their comfort zone. Two years after the company went burst many were still unemployed and unable to find new jobs even though there were alternative better jobs that they could get.

What was happening to them? They were unable to break free from a comfort zone that no longer served them. I have met graduates who after years of searching for the job they really want settles for something they called "temporary" just to get the bills paid. 10 years later, what was temporary is now permanent and even when they lose the temporary job they are no longer able to look for opportunities in new industries; they continue to search for jobs in industries similar to the ones they classified as temporary.

How many people return to old relationships, not because they expect any change in the relationship, but rather it is what they have become familiar with. How many more are living in towns and cities that they thought were temporary when they visited an uncle, but ten years down the line, what was temporary is now permanent?

In 2003 I sold everything I owned to do a full time MBA. It was costly, risky and a big dive. It was one of those decisions that I embarked on to break the habits that defined my boundaries. I was getting interested in management, but I graduated in Civil Engineering from the University of Benin and was working as a Structural engineer in a construction firm. To really make sure I changed, I decided to embrace something new. After selling everything I could sell, I was able to raise 20% of the fees, and off I went to University College, Dublin, and Republic of Ireland.

In a class of nearly 50 working adults from 24 different countries, a survey taken by the university Careers Director showed that 95% of students who had come to the program wanted career change and another 80% wanted to migrate to a new country. The career changes many of us were seeking bothered around leaving operational roles for a managerial role, leaving banking for consulting, moving from commercial banking to investment banking.

Somehow in my class, the vast majority wanted investment banking roles in London or joining one of the big names like Apple, Dell, Amazon and so forth which were the delight of most **MBA** students as of 2003. I was a structural engineer and wanted to erase that tag by moving into something completely different -either Investment Banking or one of the big names. I did everything I could to get headway, but only succeeded in getting to the finals of being interviewed for a finance leadership position at Dell European Headquarters in Dublin.

Finally, in desperation, I set aside my **MBA** and took a job in Dublin as a Structural Engineer. About 2 years later, I will later find out that over 80% of those who yearned to use the **MBA** to make a career change or change their country of residence for a new experience did not succeed at it, at least not immediately.

Nearly 20 years later, as I learn about breaking habits and exiting the familiar, I am trying to find clues as to why many of us went back to the familiar. We were four structural engineers in the class of **MBA** 2004. Two years after graduation, all four of us were back working as structural engineers. While I failed in my push to move to a finance role, I at least succeeded in changing the country I worked - from Nigeria to Ireland.

What could we have really done to actualize the changes we so desired? What can really get a person out of the familiar into the unfamiliar? How can a person get past a relationship going nowhere and yet stuck after repeated failures? What is it that lures us to the familiar and keeps us away from vast new uncontested territories and how might we break out of these limitations?

Chapter Thirty-two

BOEING 737 MAX
A Mind Trying to Overpower its Owner.

> *I do not understand what I do. For what
> I want to do I do not do, but what
> I hate I do. For I have the desire to do
> what is good, but I cannot carry it out.
> "* – Rm 7: 15 -24 **Apostle Paul**

The Boeing Max 737 is supposed to be one of the most advanced aircrafts from Boeing. Unfortunately, the fleet is grounded, production stopped. There are over 5,000 orders placed for the aircraft and Boeing has only been able to deliver 350. As advanced and sleek as it is, it recorded two fatal crashes in October 2018 and in March 2019. What caused an aircraft so advanced in every way to record two fatalities in a span of 5 months? The software refused instructions.

In a previous chapter, I wrote on Artificial intelligence (**AI**) and how our mind works like artificial intelligence and how this intelligence powers most of our life. I will extract a portion of this previous post here,

"This **AI** is very powerful and makes a lot of decisions for us that we are not even aware of". **Marianne Szegedy-Maszak**, writing for the **US News and World Report** has this to say,

"According to cognitive neuroscientists, we are conscious of only about 5 percent of our cognitive activity, so most of our decisions, actions, emotions, and behaviour depend on the 95 percent of brain activity that goes beyond our conscious awareness".

"If you drive regularly, I am sure that you have had the experience of driving a few kilometres and unaware of when and how you did it. What was happening was that your **AI** just took control and gave the instructions on the lane to take, the speed to go at and what else you needed to do. How is the **AI** able to do this? When you were driving that route for the first time and repeatedly, you wrote mental programs of how to get through the route – you coded your brain. Once your **AI** got the code, he didn't really need you again" – (I recommend you read the whole article on **AI** published previously).

My friend Kingsley Oghoyon Ik talked about being led astray by his mind and absconding to the **US** on a spurious fear for his life when he was threatened by a supposed business acquaintance in Lagos, Nigeria. With his permission, I am reproducing part of his confessions here. "….I was in a mind made prison, I ran away to the **US** for six months; when my wife and kids saw me upon my return, they were shocked, I was a shadow of myself. However, within those six months, I was able to free myself of the mind made prison.

The mind is powerful, it can **EXAGGERATE** issues if you let it wander, it can build, and it can destroy. One must pray to have the ability to see beyond dark thoughts, the light and life after every dark tunnel is greater than the former". I can relate with this story as I have been a victim of this mind made prison on more than one occasions. My mind exaggerated a situation at work to such an extent that I was even afraid to go to work. With help from my then boss, who told me to take a few days off, I was able to recover myself.

The point of this chapter is to give you the tools to fight that "prison" that is trying to lead you in a direction that you do not wish to go. That "prison" was built by you, but you built it in ignorance. You did not build it to destroy you. You built it to serve as your guardian angel. Imagine this, 67% of a child's self-esteem is already formed by the time the child is 5. At that age, a child does not even know what self-esteem is about.

Later in life the child is struggling with a poor self-esteem and we only look at the fact that the child, now grown up has 1st class from the University, but we are unable to unearth the environment the child grew up in the first 5 years and how, to survive, he/she had to code the AI to protect him/her in a manner that looked best.

As Marianne Szegedy said above, we are not even conscious of 95% of the decisions we are making. Artificial Intelligence as distinct from computing, once you have given it guidelines, it starts to make its own set of rules. The danger occurs when it makes decisions based on an erroneous judgement. In the 2 Boeing crashes, the pilots fought unsuccessfully to stop the **AI** from flying the plane, but they could not.

I have read a few stories on suicides, I can tell you with 99% degree of certainty, and the **AI**s took control and just ran the persons aground. I followed the press reports of some murder cases. In 99% of the cases where the murderer was arrested alive, he/she is crying after just a month in detention. He/she cannot even believe they did it.

What is the way out of this mind made prison? The way out, is first to know the forces that are at play here. The 5% conscious control over your affairs is very powerful. That 5% is like an Army General commanding 19 other subordinate soldiers. On a % basis, he is just 5% of the troupe, but his decision overrides all the other 20 subordinate officers put together. But if he does not know what to do, he will ask for a vote and he will be overpowered.

The first step to freedom is to realize that some software you wrote a long time is trying to dictate your life. Several years before you got married, you wrote a code on what it means to be loved. Now you are married, and you are finding it difficult to see that android and mac are incompatible software and that a new one needs to be written that will take some parts of android and mac. A great part of this program you even wrote when you were not thinking of marriage, like the child with 67% self-esteem already set by age 5.
Once this knowledge sinks in, you may now need to challenge this program that is trying to make you exit your marriage. Elizabeth Taylor married eight times. You will have to consciously implant a new programming. Is it easy? To tell you the truth, this is the real fight of life. Like Boeing pilots fighting a program trying to take over a flight, you must put up a fight. See what the great apostle Paul said in the Bible, "… I am doing what I hate to do…"

I have no intention to be depressed, but I wake up depressed every morning. I never thought I will be this gloomy because I was laid off work, but here I am, unable to even laugh with my kids. Your AI is trying to run your life. This AI is a fully-grown man, now you are going to speak to him and tell him that you are not going to obey him anymore. Even when a person is suicidal or murderous, psychology has it that at the minimum, 5% of him is against that thought. With this knowledge, such a person now knows what is at play, he or she should revolt against those subordinate armies of thoughts and take control. An alternative to speaking to the thought is to simply watch these tormenting thoughts and **DO NOTHING**.

I remember trying to fast for the first time, once it was 11am; my body told me he was hungry. For an entire week, my weeklong fast ended by 11am daily. Why? Because I ceded my command to my **AI**. One day I got to 1pm and the shop next door where they sell fried rice was preparing rice. I cried for 1 hour fighting to resist the pull of the rice, but I failed, I went for it.

One day, I told my **AI** I will not obey him again when it came to fasting. I crossed 11am, 1pm; the neighbours fried rice and got to 5pm. Do this repeatedly and what you have done is that you have amended the programming and your **AI** will use this new program next time.

Are you under pressure to be depressed? Suicidal? Or anything in between? You are the General of your life. You are going to marshal out the greatest military mental and spiritual energy and arrest that software that no longer serves your interest. Your interests have changed, that coding must be upgraded.

Many of us are not conscious of this programming, so repeatedly we think software that we wrote when we were 2 years old is who we are. Check your laptop or smart phone, it is updating every now and then. I was talking to a guy who was in a conflict with his in-laws recently and I asked him if he thought it was worth dropping his thoughts for just an hour and fantasizing with the opinions of his in-law?

He replied that his in-law would have to make do with who he is. When I told him that he wasn't who he thought he is, he still could not get it. This is where knowledge comes in. You will have to wrestle control from a timidity that you grew up with. The problem with many of us is that we have come to build our identity around a set of beliefs that we wrote when we didn't know what we were doing. We must now amend this programming if we are to enjoy life to the fullest.

Chapter Thirty-three

You are not your Thoughts

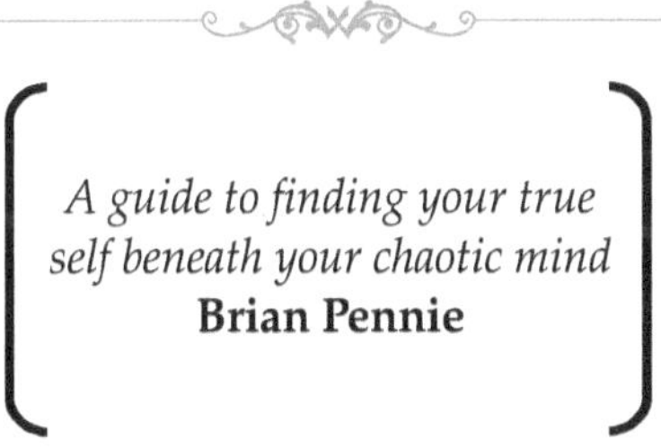

Eckhart Tolle is a spiritual teacher and author of The Power of Now, widely regarded as one of the most influential spiritual books of our time. At the age of 29, he experienced a profound inner transformation that radically changed the course of his life.

One night, not long after his 29th birthday, he woke up in the early hours with a feeling of absolute dread. He had previously battled with anxiety and suicidal depression, but it was more intense than ever before, and he began to question his reason for living. As he played with the idea of suicide, the same thought kept repeating itself in his mind:

"I cannot live with myself any longer."

He suddenly became aware of what a peculiar thought this was. "Am I one or two? If I cannot live with myself, there must be two of me: the 'I' and the 'self'… maybe only one of them is real."

He was so stunned by this bizarre realization that his mind stopped.

He was fully conscious, but there were no more thoughts. He was then drawn into what seemed like a vortex of energy and could feel himself being sucked in. Suddenly, there was no more fear, and he let himself fall into the void.

Upon waking the following day, the world seemed very different. Although he recognized the room, he had never truly seen it. Everything looked fresh and alive as if it had just come into existence. He knew something profound had occurred, but didn't understand what it was. It wasn't until several years later that he realized what had happened. The intense suffering of that night had forced a split in his consciousness. His deeply fearful 'self' fell away, and all that was left was the ever-present 'I'.

The 'I' and the 'self'

Are you your thoughts? Are you your feelings? Are you your body, or bodily sensations?

No. You are none of these. How can you be if they are always changing?

Do you feel different now than you did last week? Do you have different thoughts today than when you were in school? Do you look different now than you did 10 years ago?

Of course, you do, but the same person is still looking in the mirror, the same person is thinking those thoughts, and the same person is feeling those feelings.

Your thoughts, feelings and body make up your 'self-concept', but this is not who you truly are. You are the observer, the ever-present 'I', the one who observes the 'self'.

Self-Observation

If I asked you to focus on your body or bodily sensations, it's likely that you'd focus on a specific area, such as your breath, pulse, or chest.

If I asked you what you were thinking, you can observe this too. You might be planning for the week ahead, or worrying about money, but it's possible to take a step back and observe these thoughts.

It's the same for feelings. If I asked you how you feel, you could take a step back and observe how you feel.

The point is, you can take an observer's perspective of your thoughts, feelings and bodily sensations.

The floating clouds metaphor describes this best:

Imagine your thoughts, feelings or bodily sensations as clouds floating through the sky. Sometimes they're dark and angry; sometimes they're light and calm. But you are not the clouds. You are the blue sky who observes the clouds, without engaging. You simply observe them until they pass, and they will pass. Everything passes, good and bad. Be the blue sky.

Be the observer.

Why is this important?

Many people are anxious and overwhelmed without realizing why. But it doesn't have to be this way. Next time you feel agitated or uneasy; take a few minutes to mindfully observe your thoughts, feelings and bodily sensations.

If you feel anxious, don't engage. Just observe the feelings and let them pass. When you have uncomfortable thoughts, don't let them define you - let them pass. If you have uncomfortable bodily sensations, accept them as they are, and let them pass. Don't engage. Be the observer.

If you practice this regularly, you will create a sense of detachment when challenging situations arise. You will still feel it in your body, but there will be a space, and instead of feeling stressed or overwhelmed, you will be able to respond in a rational manner.

All You Need to Know

You are not your thoughts, feelings or physical body. This is your self-concept, which is simply who you think you are.

When I suffered from anxiety many years ago I used to call it 'my anxiety'. I felt anxious all the time. This was my self-concept. I turned to drugs to cope with 'my anxiety'. I looked like and thought of myself as an addict. These were the thinking and physical aspects of my self-concept.

As far as I was concerned, I was an unhealthy looking anxious addict. And yes, this was a fairly accurate description, but it was not my true self, not who I really was. I don't suffer from anxiety anymore, and I don't think of myself as an addict, so how could that have been who I truly was.

I certainly don't have Eckhart Tolle's peace of mind, but when difficult situations arise, there is a space, and I respond in a rational manner.

This is the power of self-observation.

What would you do if you had a second chance at life?

Having escaped from the depths of heroin addiction, I decided to devour every second of it. Then I decided to write a book about it.

Bonus Time: A true story of surviving the worst and discovering the magic of every moment.

Chapter THIRTY-FOUR

Breaking The Habit of Being Yourself
– For Things to Change, you have to Change

> *A new year means nothing*
> *unless you have a new mind*
> *– TD Jakes*

In the last 10 years, I have had the privilege of working with three security guards in Nigeria who are part time students in the university. I am so thrilled to see these hard-working men undertake pursuits that have tremendous potential to transform their lives. The first of these 3 persons has finished **NYSC**, I have lost contact with him. The second, Dapo, is currently in his final year studying Political Science at the Lagos State University – I have maintained contact with him for the last 6 years and occasionally, providing him with whatever support that I can give. He is partly the inspiration of this chapter.

Some months ago, I wanted a loose personal assistant to pick up the slacks in occasional surges in my private life, especially surges of the type that take a lot of time rather than intellect; activities that use up so much time on the traffic, house repairs, filling forms at Government offices, picking up a cheque book from the bank, finding special products in the market place, etc.

After telling my wife that I wanted to take a serving **NYSC** corps member or freshly mint college graduate to run these time-consuming errands, she suggested Dapo. Although, Dapo does a lot for me and her in activities that require a lot of physical energies, I just could not mentally come to terms with the idea of sending Dapo to Zenith bank to pick up a cheque book.

It is six years now since I have known Dapo and for all of these six years, he has worked as a security guard for three different friends and offices close to where I live in Lagos. He is hardworking, honest and loyal. When he was in 300L, he lost his job because the family he worked for moved to Canada and he came asking me if I needed a security guard. A few weeks after, he got a job as a security guard with another friend.

As I reflected on my refusal to hire Dapo for this role, I said to my wife, "a university degree isn't all that changes a destiny".

I counted my words, paused as I said these words. How can I say this when I have been an advocate of education as the panacea to every societal ill for over a decade?

Then these words came out of my mouth, "for Dapo to use his degree in Political Science, he must break the habits that have come to define him, and this is the hardest part of life". I know nothing more difficult for any mortal than breaking the habits that define him/her.

Dr Joe Dispenza has an excellent book from where the words, "breaking the habits of being you" leaped out of my mouth. I have listened to the audio of the book, it is scientifically sound, but putting it into practice is **HARD WORK**.

In 2003, it seemed like I was going in circles. I was running a small construction company and doing fine caring for my family, but like Dapo, I wanted more out of my life. I attended every possible seminar I could find in Lagos, but I could not stretch myself out of doing only small construction projects.

I knew people who were not half as knowledgeable as me in construction doing a hundred times the size of the projects I was doing. I wanted these kinds of jobs, but for whatever reasons, I just never came close to doing any of these. As I studied and read voraciously, I concluded that the outcome of a man's life is more a product of the size of his thoughts than his academic qualifications.

Although this conclusion has remained true to me for over 20 years now, I still don't have a simple go-to strategy by which a person might alter his thoughts. While these thoughts roamed freely in my mind, my good friend who is now Lagos State Commissioner for Economic planning and Budget, Sam Egube came visiting and told me about the quantum leap he experienced as a student at the Lagos Business School.

He told me the fees, but it looked too much for my fledging business to afford. He decided to go one step further, he gave me a personal cheque for 50% of the fees, the amount needed for me to be admitted to the 4 months part time Advanced Management Program (**AMP-12**) of the Lagos Business School, and off I went to school.

My experience at the Lagos Business School beats what words can really describe. It was life changing and it ignited a deep hunger in me. Two years later that hunger continued to burn, and I decided to do a full time **MBA** at the University College, Dublin.

It is obvious that my mind was growing. Somehow, you don't really know in the very moment if your mind has changed. Mind growth, I found out isn't really something you notice in the moment. Sometimes it is so small that you don't even think anything happened. I learned from motivational speaker, Jim Rohn, that a small change of 2 degrees in mind can have very profound life changing impact on our lives.

Draw a triangle and with the angle to the horizontal set at just 2 degrees. Imagine that the horizontal is time and the vertical axis is the change in your life; when you project it over 20 years, you will see that your life has changed by over 200% what it would have been without this new knowledge acted upon.

Does every new knowledge bring about a quantum change in life? The answer as you might have rightly guessed is **NO**. The only knowledge that changes your life is the one you act upon. This, in my personal life is where the challenge is. To recant the now popular quote, "it is insanity to do the same thing and expect a different outcome".

If Dapo has been attending the Lagos State University part time program for 3 years that new knowledge has the capacity to elevate his life to a different kind of job, but he has to act on it. You might say, he has not gotten a job that fares better than a night guard. You see, that isn't true. Jobs don't come to anyone of their own accord. All jobs are mentally created or embraced first before they become reality in our lives.

The reality is that his habits have him hardwired to be a security guard. Additional knowledge gained in the university just means increased store of knowledge, not a change of life circumstance. But he is not in school for increased store of knowledge; he is in school for a change of life circumstances. In a way, he would need to say **NO** to the old for the new to come in.

Reconciling these two contradictory positions is what "Breaking the habit of being yourself is all about". To transition from a security guard to a graduate job, Dapo must "Break the habit of who he is". I know nothing more difficult than doing this. It is easier to go to the moon than to break the ingrained habits that have come to define your personality. But if you are tired of the life you now live, you will take the plunge.

The older you get the more difficult it is to change your personality. In certain cases, it looks impossible. What will you do if you were the man by the pool of Bethesda that Jesus talked about in the bible? For 38 years, you have sat by this pool with other sick people like you and helpers who gave you food.

Your brain knew **ONLY ONE WAY** to get healed – "the first person that jumped into the water, after it was stirred by an angel". But you hear of Jesus and that He can make you whole without waiting for an angel to stir up the waters. You intellectually believe it, but you just cannot see how this can take place. Then Jesus walks up to you and asks you if you want to be made whole? What is your response? The same that many of us will give today.

You know that the economy is not good and graduate jobs are few. Covid 19 is ravaging the economy and there is nothing that anyone can do. That is what Dapo has said to himself all these years and has remained a guard. The man goes on with his stories,

"look Jesus, I have no man and every time I even make attempt, I am never the first to get into the water, so I have even stopped trying. I pay someone to push me into the water and when I am not the first, I drink some more water and pay more to be brought out. This life is so frustrating and unfair". What do you think the man is looking for?

New knowledge. But what does he really need? To be made **WHOLE**! What did Jesus do? He ignored his stories, and told him, "rise, take up thy bed and walk".

How can a man who is crippled **RISE**? I think this is the crux of breaking the habit of who we are. 38 years of knowing only one way to get healed, 4 years of knowing only one way of travelling abroad, 6 years of knowing only one way of getting a job, twelve years of knowing only one way of getting married and on and on the list goes.

How do we ditch these ingrained hardwired patterns of behaviours and embrace a new reality? In Dr Joe Dispenza's book, "Breaking the habit of being yourself", the subtitle reads "How to lose your mind and create a new one".

Chapter Thirty-five

Finding Your Way Out of
Caught up Thinking Avenue

There is an avenue called **CAUGHT UP AVENUE**. This avenue can be tricky in our everyday life. I know you may think that if you ever drove into this avenue, you will switch on your Google Map or Waze App. Unfortunately, Google map or Waze cannot get you out of this avenue. Remember images of the tangled thread or rope when you were growing up? It just does not look possible that this tangled rope can be untangled; but it can with **PATIENCE AND TIME**.

When some parents find out that their young ones have tangled their thread, they think of all the difficulties it will take to untangle it and they just throw it into the dust bin. They conclude that it is not worth the effort. At some other times, considering how precious the thread is, how much it was bought, the difficulty in procuring one, a parent may consider it worthwhile to spend an entire day or days just to untangle a thread. Do you know that our thoughts are like that tangled thread? Sometimes our thoughts are so tangled that we do not even know where to start the untangling from.

The decision on whether we will invest time to untangle the thoughts or just perish with them is a thing that needs careful consideration. Like the thread analogy I gave, this decision will be based on the value of the thread to you. But there is one difference between tangled thread and tangled thoughts.

When it is an external thread, you take an objective view; but when it is your thought you are many times unable to take an objective view because of the connection between you and your thought.

This place is where Joseph Bailey & Richard Carlson calls the **CAUGHT-UP AVENUE** in their book "**SLOWING DOWN TO THE SPEED OF LIFE**". Honestly, I recommend this book to everyone. It is a personal development reference bible to me.

Our greatest delusion in life is the faulty thinking that our feelings come from anywhere **OTHER THAN OUR THINKING IN THE MOMENT**. Your feelings of pain, bitterness, anger, resentment is not coming from what your spouse did to you. They are coming from the meanings that you made from the events. It is simpler said than lived, but the moment you grasp this simple statement, **YOUR EXPERIENCE OF LIFE INSTANTLY TAKES A DIFFERENT MEANING**.

You will experience peace that is unexplainable **WITHOUT** any changes to your life circumstances. And once you build this consciousness into your life, it is **THE BEGINNING** of bye-bye to any relationship pain the remaining days of your life. You meet a beautiful lady and you lose your breath just gazing at her, you motion to know her more, but as you listen to her, you find that inside is not beautiful. What is the matter you wonder? The matter is that all of our life experiences are internally self-created.

When I said the girl was beautiful, maybe you thought there was a universal standard for beauty, there is none. She was beautiful judging by the set of criteria I have come to define beauty with. She is reeling out bitterness and regrets because life doesn't seem to be going with the set of criteria that she set in her memory. Sometimes, we can get so caught up in these painful thoughts that we lose our way. Micheal Neil, author of the "The Space Within" writes on how to **FIND YOUR WAY BACK HOME**. When you get caught up in too many tangled thoughts, you have propelled your life into **CAUGHT UP AVENUE**. What you now need to do is to find your way back home.

The fact that you are caught up in your thinking is more relevant to the way you feel than to the specific details of whatever you are caught up about. That doesn't mean that what you are concerned about isn't important, the question is, are you thinking about the problem from a healthy psychological place or from frenetic, troubled state of mind? Given that thoughts and feelings are one and the same, the more caught up you are, the more you are going to feel worse.

You will imagine your problems to be **BIGGER** than they actually are and with **NO SOLUTION**. You get busy and you accomplish **NOTHING**. Your mind is running from Alaska to Pretoria from what was done to you 20 years ago to something that can happen tomorrow. You forget that all of these evil **MACHINATIONS** exist **ONLY** in one place – **YOUR THOUGHTS**. But the reality is that **YOU ARE NOT YOUR THOUGHTS AND YOUR THOUGHTS ARE NOT REALITY.**

All of our experience of life are thought created. They were made up by us. The thinking that you are not enjoying your marriage is all made up by **YOU**. And so too is the thinking that you are enjoying your marriage. The difference in the two states is that one is tormenting you while the other is generating happy feelings. In state one, you will not have sex with your spouse tonight. It is just impossible. Thoughts and feelings go together.

The internal meanings you made about your spouse shouting like a dog at you yesterday just cannot bring you near anything called sex. But in a different mood, you know he shouts like a dog anyway but you don't take them personal anymore, that is his business and you have even come to find out that when you have sex with him just after he has shouted like a dog it is so enjoyable and he becomes remorseful.

One kind of thinking that can aggravate you when you are in **CAUGHT UP AVENUE** is the kind of thinking called "**BLACK AND WHITE**" thinking. Oh, how I hate this thinking. I have been a victim of this thinking severally, in the workplace and in family life. This thinking sees only two possibilities; it is either black or white. Either the marriage is working, or we are divorced. This kind of thinking can send you to the psychiatrist's.

Life does not come in black and white; it comes in several shades and sometimes, unfamiliar to our mental wiring. I learnt this the hard way. When you think of life in just **BLACK AND WHITE**, you are going to experience extremes of behaviour in most relationships you find yourself. You will be swift to judge others because to you, life is either black or white.

Google the phrase "**BLACK AND WHITE THINKING**", you see plenty of information on this subject. A relationship cannot be judged to be a failure just based on one-character flaw. I have quit jobs because I looked at the organization in **BLACK AND WHITE THINKING** only to find out years later that I was wrong. I remember one case where I wrote to withdraw my resignation, but alas, the CEO will not give me a second chance.

I was like Esau in Hebrews 12:17, when he sought the blessing he earlier repudiated with tears but could not get it again. Esau saw things only in black and white. Either I get porridge or my birth right. If he looked at life from several shades of flavours he would have known how to get both his birth right and his porridge meal.

When I think about leadership, **David** and his army commander **Joab** comes to mind. On the face of their contrariness these two people should not work together, but you see, Joab was David's army chief until the death of David. Here is a man who will behind David arrange to kill the very people that David was in covenant with. On more than 3 different occasions, Joab executed persons that David warned him not to touch. Yet, this same Joab defended David like none other until the death of David.

If you want to learn how to think in 50 shades of grey, study the life of Joab and David in second Kings. You will be humbled. Joab will rout an enemy army and send for David to come stand as the one who defeated the army lest the people begin to chant him Joab as the hero. When David commanded that no harm should be done to his son Absalom, Joab smote and killed Absalom. Severally, they both cried when one did what the other did not want, but they remained unbroken brothers at war for over 50 years. Talk about 50 shades of grey.

One thing that I bring out from the story is that they both knew the individual values that each person brought to the relationship. When we are in caught up avenue, we do not see the values that our partners bring to our lives; these values have been shrouded in our **THINKING IN THE MOMENT**. But we can untangle these hard-wired thinking and begin to enjoy our everyday lives. It takes a great deal of **SLOWING DOWN TO THE SPEED OF** LIFE to see the value that your spouse brings to the table when you are driving along caught up avenue.

 I dare say that men need a lot more humility in slowing down to recognize what their wives bring to the relationship than women. By default, men think that just being a man has given them 60% value contribution to a relationship even if all you do for the rest of your life is watch super sports. This is not true. But I also dare say to women that your job is not to correct this erroneous thinking; learn how to create healthy meanings with your thought life and the absurdity of that kind of thinking in men will gradually fade away.

When you are in caught up avenue, instead of enjoying the moment with your other half, you are analysing their actions. In black and white thinking, you must beware of the following dangers – premature decision making, lack of compromise, unrealistic expectations, and unhealthy boundaries. A quote from Michael Patanella reads "We are moulded, and evolved, to travel through life looking away from ourselves whenever there is an issue.

We can't go through life holding mirrors in front of ourselves, as we wrongly go about trying to pinpoint what entity is fooling all our real-life issues. Well, we can ourselves be guilty. Even if we are not the problem, maybe we have to take a step back and remember that we are not our thoughts, and just because we think it, doesn't mean it's true".

If this chapter has met you while driving through **CAUGHT UP AVENUE**, you can try some of these suggestions to find your way back home.

1) **SHIFT YOUR THINKING** – As soon as you realize that you are the **THINKER** and that your thought making machine works independent of the circumstance and can magnify any circumstance, shift your energy to a different place in time.

2) **SLOW DOWN AND STRECTH TIME** – It takes a lot of work to untangle a tangled thread. When your mind is rushing to what can happen 5 years from now, slow down and go play some football, life should be lived **IN THE MOMENT**. There is nothing called tomorrow.

3) Move from "**BLACK AND WHITE THINKING**" TO "**50 SHADES OF GREY**". If you have studied complex negotiations like Brexit or the China – America trade conflict, you will see that to **LEAD**, you must know how to think in 50 shades of grey. In one dimension, Russia is an enemy of the United States, yet on another dimension the two countries are working together to solve a problem. To a person who thinks black and white, this is impossible. Welcome to the higher life.

Chapter Thirty-six

To Succeed, you must ACTIVATE your Multiple Personalities

> *You can take on any personality at any time. Everyone has multiple personalities that together will make every limitation to give way.*

I wasted too many years waiting to feel something before taking action. I lost several business and entrepreneurial opportunities. I will lie on the bed waiting for one strange feeling called passion to suddenly fall on me before doing what I knew would be of benefit to me. An opportunity to take action will stand naked before me and I will let it slip because the feeling for action did not come. I blamed my inaction on my personality.

I was born a shy person, I am an introvert, it did not feel good to talk too confidently, blah, blah, and blah. So much junk spewing out of me at the time. It is only proud people that talk that way. Having big dreams was not godly after all. I had so many excuses that helped support and encourage the building of a personality that I called **ME**.

When I saw friends and relatives take on different personalities, my internal dialogue labelled them as being ungodly, fake and hypocrites. As a teenager, I remember attending a religious gathering where the minister spoke so pious and I wondered how he could be this way with his wife and kids.

It just doesn't look possible that this man has a wife; no man can possibly talk like this and be able to have sex. It just wasn't real except he was a different person on the pulpit from what he was at home. I look back and wonder how I must have been quite "stupid" to think like this. Like it or not, that was me then and that was the ignorant me.

I am right to think that the priest must put on a new personality when he is about making love to his wife, the problem was I just did not know that I too was putting on different personalities for different occasions. When I sang in the choir, I was a different person from the one that was sleeping or running. When I thought my friends were fake because they wore different personalities for different occasions, it did not occur to me that I too was fake. In fact, in retrospect, I was the real **FAKE**, not them.

They knew something I did not know, they knew that as humans we all have plenty personalities living inside of us and that the skilful act of living demands that we activate the personality that was appropriate for the moment. While I activated different personalities for different occasions, I foolishly thought that personality was a fixed steel structure, not knowing that I was fixated on just one of several possibilities that I lived in. Donald Trump is the president of the United States. That is one personality. At home, he is a father and a husband.

Today I see so many persons, especially young adults who have come to identify themselves with just one personality – a fixed statue in their minds akin to the statue of liberty in New York. They relate with this invisible persona that lives only within their imagination. They are not aware that this statue that they have created does not exist. In my work as speaker and coach, I had a session with a young adult a few weeks ago and this was the way a part of the conversation went:

Me: Can you tell me why you turned down the sales offer from Microsoft?

Mr D: My uncle in New York got the job for me, I will never go for a sales job knowing who I am and my personality type

Me: Can you enlighten me on who you are and your personality type?

Mr D: I am an introvert, I rarely socialize. My parents can testify to this and I have been this way since I was born. I guess one's personality is acquired from birth.

Me: That thing you call your personality does not exist. It is a creation of you, your thinking, and your imagination. I thought this way for a long time, I thought I was an introvert and I was condemned to die this way. I avoided a great deal of social interactions because I felt I was a shy person. I wasted "time without end" to get myself into action once it involved even making a simple sales call. One day, I found out that all my life experiences are only thought created. It was a eureka moment for me.

Mr D: So, you mean I can change my personality? How long do you think it will take?

Me: I mean you have different personalities right now and you can use your thoughts to decide which one you wish to project right now. It is not something that requires 10,000 hours of practice. It is something that you can do right now. You see, we all project different personalities every day. Have you watched Black Panther?

Mr D: Yes, I have

Me: You see Chadwick Boseman had to activate a new personality. The personality that you activate depends on the occasion. That is why actors can take on different roles. Chadwick is not ruling Wakanda when he gets home, but to play the role he had to wear a new personality. That you hardly go to social gatherings doesn't mean that you cannot do it, it just means you chose not to, and that is because you are thinking thoughts that make you not to. What you need to do is just take on a new thinking, **NOW**

Mr D: "silence"

Me: Who would you be if you did not have the thoughts that you are thinking right now? I tell you the truth, you will be totally invisible, **THERE IS NOTHING THAT WILL BE IMPOSSIBLE FOR YOU TO DO**. You see, all experiences of life are self-created through thoughts, so are all **LIMITATIONS**. We limit ourselves without thinking. By design, we were designed to be impregnable, godlike, with ability to create and bring into being whatever we can think or imagine, but the very tool that God gave us to create **WHATEVER WE WANT**, we have turned around to build silos that have imprisoned us. If you understand what I am talking about, you will wake up tomorrow morning and ask to be the chief marketing officer of Microsoft.

Mr D: Thank you very much sir, I am calling my uncle right away and I will be taking up the job and resuming immediately.

Me: You are welcome Mr D, feel free to call me anytime.

In the course of my public speaking and coaching activities, I have painfully encountered so many young adults like **Mr D** who are wasting valuable potentials because they are waiting for a feeling to take action, when really, they should be doing the reverse. The feelings will come when you **TAKE ACTION**. You feel what you think, you do not think what you feel. The feeling follows the thinking. It always works this way. So, do not wait to feel like you are not shy before you take an action, just replace the shy thoughts with thoughts that make you a lion and shyness is all history.

Of all the great autobiographies and biographies, I have read (and I have read a lot), over 75% of the successful billionaires, politicians, preachers and executives say that they grew up as **introverts**. Somewhere in their story, they found out either consciously or unconsciously that personality was not a fixed concrete structure. They changed personalities as the occasion served them.
I remember listening to the great preacher, Kenneth Copeland; in the beginning days of his ministry, he will start his preaching with his tape recorder on and immediately after the preaching go to the back stage and change his suit and come out selling audio tapes of the message he just preached. In 10 minutes, the preacher has turned out to be a salesman. You too can do this.

Rather than wait "forever" for a feeling to do what you know you ought to be doing right now, what you need is the knowledge that every personality type exists inside you right now. The one you call your personality is the one that you decided to be fixated upon. With this understanding, you can now call upon any personality that you need as the occasion demands.

Some years ago, a friend arranged for me to be appointed into a very high-profile executive role. It did not occur to me that I should find out the personality required for this role. At this high-profile interview and in front of some very prominent executives, I projected a personality that was wrong for the job. It was like being interviewed to play the role of Chadwick Boseman in Black Panther and showing a personality of a monk. I guess you know the outcome of that interview, I was **NEVER** taken and was not even given a second chance.

Quantum science is beginning to show that all possibilities exist in every person; kind of telling us something Jesus said in the scriptures. All things are possible. Which possibility you give expression to in your life is dependent on your choices. Activate the right personality for the appropriate moment and you or **ANYONE CAN DO IT AT ANY TIME**.

ACTION ALWAYS TRUMPS THINKING – TAKE ACTION

THE END.

About the Author

Tunde Ekpekurede, **MBA** is an authority in the field of mental toughness and resilience and has served as speaker, facilitator, and executive coach in this field for over a decade. He has worked in executive level positions in the Republic of Ireland, Northern Ireland, England, and Nigeria.

An Alumni of the Smurfit Graduate School of Business, University College, Dublin where he obtained his **MBA** (2004), and the Lagos Business School (2001), he graduated from the University of Benin with honours in Civil Engineering in 1989 and obtained a certificate in Project Management from Harvard University, Boston **USA** in 2012.

A consummate reader and writer, his writings are available on several print and digital media including medium. His interest is to support individuals and organizations in the attainment of their potentials.